MW00586545

Sister Thea Bowman,
Shooting Star

Sister Thea Bowman, Shooting Star:

Selected Writings and Speeches

Edited by Celestine Cepress, FSPA
Foreword by Mike Wallace

Saint Mary's Press
Christian Brothers Publications
Winona, Minnesota

The publishing team for this book included Carl Koch, FSC, development editor; Rebecca Fairbank, copy editor; Barbara Bartelson, production editor and typesetter; Tara Christopherson/Fruitful Results, cover designer; pre-press, printing, and binding by the graphics division of Saint Mary's Press.

The back cover illustration *Rise Up Shepherd and Follow,* by Michael O'Neill McGrath, is from the series "The Transformations of Sister Thea Bowman."

The cover and inside photographs are from the Franciscan Sisters of Perpetual Adoration archives. They are used with permission.

The acknowledgments continue on page 135.

Copyright © 1993 by Saint Mary's Press, 702 Terrace Heights, Winona, MN 55987-1320. All rights reserved. No part of this book may be reproduced by any means without the written permission of the publisher.

Printed in the United States of America

Printing: 9 8 7 6 5 4 3 2 1

Year: 2001 00 99 98 97 96 95 94 93

ISBN 0-88489-302-2

To the Elders of Canton, Mississippi, past and present
who taught Thea
        that old-time religion
        how to share life, faith, and love
        how to sing the songs of faith
who told Thea
        to preach the Gospel to the whole world
        that black is beautiful
        that she had a heritage to pass on
        to never retire from the service of God
        that the glue binding us all together is love.

❦ **Contents** ❦

ᕴᕽ **Foreword** ᕴᕽ

I don't remember when I've been more moved, more enchanted by a person whom I've profiled, than by Sister Thea Bowman. I confess I was a little skeptical when she was first suggested to me by Paul and Holly Fine, the documentarians who introduced us, but just one session with this remarkable individual convinced me; her openness, her compassion, her intelligence, her optimism, her humor captured me. You simply couldn't come away from a session with Sister Thea without sharing the special sense of joy she seemed to bring to everything she turned her hand to.

And when I went with her to her hometown of Canton, Mississippi, I began to understand her even better, for I realized the long, long journey she had taken from this segregated small town where black Catholic sisters were unheard of.

This is how I introduced her on the profile we filmed for "60 Minutes" back in 1987:

> Thea Bowman was born a Protestant in Canton, Mississippi. At the age of twelve, she startled her parents with the news that she was going to become a Catholic. A few years later, she delivered even more shocking news: she would become a nun. . . .
>
> Today at forty-nine, Sister Thea is still shaking people up, preaching in her African robes, not the traditional white Catholic litany, but a new black Catholic Gospel powered by the conviction that when something is wrong, you change it.

Sister Thea worked with the old and the young. Her youngsters, the students she taught in Canton, adored her, and so did the surprised priests at Xavier College in New Orleans, whom she taught how to get closer to their parishioners.

"I tried to get them to work with their bodies," she told me. "Many of our priests in their training for preaching didn't do much body work, so techniques of relaxation, techniques of rhythm, techniques of communication and expression that come from us in the black community, that is what they have to learn to be more comfortable with." And her priestly acolytes did, on camera, for us.

Halfway into our filming, I learned that Sister Thea was already fighting cancer, but I couldn't believe it, for she was so confident, so optimistic, so determined.

"I think one difference between me and some other people is that I'm content to do my little bit. Sometimes people think they have to do big things in order to make change, but if each one of us would light a candle we'd have a tremendous light."

"But there aren't enough Sister Theas around," I told her. "One's enough," she promptly answered, "you ask my friends. They'll tell you that's plenty."

She was wrong. For I was one of her friends, and we need so many more like Sister Thea.

Mike Wallace
CBS News
"60 Minutes"

Preface

When Trinity Missionary Fr. John Ford asked his longtime friend what he was to say at her funeral, Sister Thea answered: "Just say what Sojourner Truth said about her own eventual dying. Tell them what Sojourner Truth said: 'I'm not going to die. I'm going home like a shooting star'" ("A Shooting Star," *Trinity Missions* [Winter 1990]: 5).

To anyone who knew her, Thea Bowman was a star. This book brings together selected writings and transcripts of her speeches in the hope that Thea will continue to instruct, inspire, and enlighten readers with her wisdom, joy, and love.

Gayda Hollnagel of the *La Crosse Tribune* probably summed up Sister Thea Bowman's charism best when she wrote:

> Right to the end, despite years of debilitating bone cancer, Thea was preaching, teaching and singing praises to her God.
>
> When Thea was around, you didn't doubt there was a God. You could see him in the warm, welcoming acceptance of her eyes.
>
> You could hear him in her clear, strong voice and in her laughter.
>
> Even with her hair gone, bald from the chemotherapy, she was a work of art in native African dress.
>
> God made her and it was all good.
>
> She made people clap their hands and sing. Even TV newsman Mike Wallace and stodgy Roman Catholic bishops were helpless against the joy that radiated from Thea.
>
> "Black is beautiful," Thea said. And it was so.
>
> In Thea's eyes, white was beautiful, too. And red. And yellow. God doesn't make junk. We are all worthy. ("New Book Recounts Life of Cherished Nun," 1 Feb. 1992)

Indeed, the selections in this book proclaim that we are all worthy. The readings are divided into six parts: autobiographical writings, reflections on black spirituality, views on black music, thoughts on family and church, instructions about the richness of all cultures, and finally, remarks about living fully. But what shines through, regardless of the topic, is the warmth of Thea's embrace, the hope of her vision, her confidence in the deep-down goodness of humankind, and her passionate commitment to life according to Jesus.

❧ Key Dates in Thea's Life ❧

1937 Bertha Bowman is born to Mary Esther (Coleman), a teacher, and Theon Edward Bowman, a doctor, in Yazoo City, Mississippi.

1947 Bertha is baptized into the Catholic church by Fr. Justin Furman, ST, and makes her first communion.

1949 Upon discovering that she cannot read after five years in a public school, Bertha's mother transfers her to the new Catholic school, Holy Child Jesus, run by the Franciscan Sisters of Perpetual Adoration.

1953 Bertha enters the Franciscan Sisters' community in La Crosse, Wisconsin.

1955 Having contracted tuberculosis, Bertha spends the year recovering at River Pines Sanatorium in Stevens Point, Wisconsin.

1956 She commences her novitiate years, taking the name Sister Thea, which means "of God."

1958 After professing her first vows, Sister Thea begins teaching at Blessed Sacrament School in La Crosse.

1961 Sister Thea teaches English and music at Holy Child Jesus Catholic High School in Canton, Mississippi.

1968 After ten years of teaching, Sister Thea undertakes graduate studies in English at the Catholic University of America.

1972 Having completed her doctorate, Sister Thea travels in Europe and studies during the summer at Oxford. Then she begins teaching at Viterbo College in La Crosse. Eventually, Thea chairs the English department and directs the Hallelujah Singers.

1978 Returning to Canton to care for her elderly parents, Thea becomes consultant (later director) of the Office of Intercultural Awareness for the Diocese of Jackson, Mississippi, and a popular speaker throughout the nation.

1980 Thea helps found the Institute of Black Catholic Studies at Xavier University in New Orleans, Louisiana; she serves on the institute faculty until 1989.

1983 The Brother James Miller, FSC, Award goes to Thea.

1984 Diagnosed with breast cancer that has spread, Sister Thea begins treatment. She continues an active schedule of speaking engagements, teaching, and performing. Both of Thea's parents die during the year.

1985 Sister Thea travels to the Forty-third International Eucharistic Congress in Nairobi, Kenya; she also visits Zimbabwe and Nigeria. The National Black Sisters' Conference recognizes Thea with the Harriet Tubman Award, and Viterbo College honors her with the Pope John XXIII Award.

1987 A segment of "60 Minutes" features Sister Thea; she is interviewed by correspondent Mike Wallace.

1988 Sister Thea conducts workshops on racism for the Maryknoll sisters in Arusha, Tanzania. Regis College in Boston awards Thea with an honorary doctorate. She subsequently receives honorary doctorates from Clarke College, Xavier University (New Orleans), Sacred Heart University, College of Our Lady of the Elms, Boston College, Georgetown University, Saint Michael's College, Marygrove College, Viterbo College, and Spring Hill College. Canton declares 23 December as Sister Thea Bowman Day. James Blanchard, governor of Michigan, recognizes Thea with the G. Mennen Williams Award.

1989 Sister Thea speaks to the annual meeting of the American bishops at Seton Hall University. She receives the *U.S. Catholic* Award for furthering the cause of women, and the Bishop Carroll T. Dozier Award from Christian Brothers College for promoting peace and justice. Saint Michael's College incorporates the Sister Thea Bowman Black Catholic Education Foundation to foster black Catholic education.

1990 Thea dies on 30 March. Funeral services are held at Holy Child Jesus Church in Canton and Saint Mary's Church in West Jackson, Mississippi. Sister Thea is buried beside her parents in Elmwood Cemetery, Memphis, Tennessee. She posthumously receives the Laetare Medal from Notre Dame University.

Part A
Thea's Story

1

Making a Joyful Noise

If we work together, pray and stand together, we can create a new heaven and ease life for each other.

Only months before Thea's death in 1990, this short autobiography was published in *CUA Magazine,* the Catholic University of America's alumni publication. In it, Sister Thea provides an outline of her life that will be filled in by the rest of her writings in this volume.

Growing up in Canton, Miss., I was what people called an "old folks' child." My parents were older, and I spent a lot of time around their friends who were grandparents and great grandparents. They made a deliberate effort to teach me about life. From their music, stories, faith, traditions and love, I learned religious, cultural and survival values. I was taught to do my best, try my hardest and keep striving up the ladder. But at each rung I was to reach back and help a brother, sister or stranger receive the gift and pass it on and thus help create a more caring, sharing world.

Although our town had segregated neighborhoods and schools and is still considered depressed because of the high proportion of poor people, I knew people who lived rich lives and continued to inspire me.

"She Inspires Thousands, but Who Inspires Her?" is reprinted from *CUA Magazine* (Winter 1990): 7–9.

One such person was "Mother" Ricker, known for her love of children. She would have 20 or 30 children at her house and would lead us in songs like "Jacob's Ladder" and "Go Down Moses." She had an unlimited repertoire of music and taught us the meaning of the words as she lived the values of the songs. Then she'd feed us and send us home happy.

Because my mother wanted me to have a chance in life, she sent me to a Catholic school. The black public schools were tremendously disadvantaged and understaffed. At the black Catholic school I remember using books given to us by St. Angela's School in Iowa and Aquinas in La Crosse, Wis. We shared gym clothes with students in Breda, Iowa. The sisters begged a lot, and because they did our school was much better supplied. Men and women all over the country gave a dollar or two to help us get an adequate education.

There were 72 of us in grades one to six, and the highest reading level was 1.7, under second-grade level. When Sister Mildred Burger became my teacher, she put me through eight levels of "Think and Do" books in one year. I was learning and enjoying it. My friends and I were challenged every day to learn and help someone else. I was poor in math, so someone had to coach me. I was good in reading, so I had to help someone else. We didn't realize it, but we were learning to cooperate and to build our community.

The priests, brothers and sisters brought an extraordinary kind of dedication to the education process. They involved us in fundraising and helped us to help ourselves. That was the key. They also worked with our parents and never left us feeling indebted. They made us feel that we contributed to the process.

It pains me to see the decline of Catholic schools in some areas of the country. Because the Catholic schools gave me a chance, I am who I am. So many of my contemporaries have achieved success as doctors, nurses, preachers, teachers, social workers, business men and women, politicians, and leaders in their communities.

When I was a high school junior in 1953, I decided to enter the convent. I had witnessed so many Catholic priests, brothers and sisters who made a difference that was far reaching. I wanted to be part of the effort to help feed the hungry, find shelter for the homeless, and teach the children.

After graduating from Viterbo College in La Crosse, Wisconsin, I taught at Catholic schools in Wisconsin and Mississippi, and then my community asked me to attend The Catholic University of America [CUA] to prepare for college-level teaching.

I had outstanding teachers at CUA including Father William J. Rooney, who was my mentor, Catherine Dunn, J. Kirby Neil, and Giovanni Giovannini. While studying literary theory, methodology, and criticism at CUA I began to realize the extent to which music encodes [the] values, history and faith of my people. While studying medieval ballads, I read an author who said the oral literary tradition no longer exists. I wrote a paper showing how the oral tradition is alive and well in the black community and how music is a way we have of preserving history and teaching values.

I received a master's degree in English in 1969 and a doctoral degree in English language and literature in 1972. The degrees helped provide many opportunities for me to share my black heritage and spirituality.

Since 1979, I have been the Diocese of Jackson's consultant for intercultural awareness and have taught at the Institute of Black Catholics at Xavier University in New Orleans, about 200 miles from Canton. I teach black theology and the arts that bring black expression to preaching, teaching and liturgy within the Church. I've spoken and sung at youth rallies, workshops and services throughout the nation, Canada and in African countries.

In 1984 I was diagnosed with breast cancer that has spread to the lymph nodes and bones. Now I'm in a wheelchair and required to travel with a companion. Because I'm subject to systemic infections, I'm not as dependable as I was a year ago.

People often ask me how I keep going. My early training is part of that ethic that enables me to do that. Old people in the black community taught us that we should serve the Lord until we die. We can even serve the Lord on our deathbeds or in any circumstances in life. If we have faith, hope and love we can pass it on.

I meet many people who do this. One I met recently is Tony Melendez of California. He is without arms but played the guitar with his toes for the pope in New Orleans. I was impressed by his faith and courage and desire to leave the world a better place.

If we work together, pray and stand together, we can create a new heaven and ease life for each other.

2

Away f'om Home

I ain't complainin', but you all can see that thisyere ain't at all like home.

At age fifteen, Bertha Bowman decided to leave her parents and nurturing black community to enter the community of sisters who taught her, the Franciscan Sisters of Perpetual Adoration. Judy Ball, writing for *Mustard Seed,* explains some of Thea's motivation:

> It was in her hometown of rural Canton, Mississippi, that Thea Bowman saw and felt the Good News in the powerful witness of the Franciscan Sisters of Perpetual Adoration. They came in the late 1940's to do there what no whites had done before: to open a school for black children, a school "in which we could get an education commensurate with our talents."
>
> The everyday niceties were few. The school itself was a reclaimed army barracks. Old orange crates served as bookcases. "But the Franciscan Sisters who came into our world," Thea recalls today, "spent quality time with us." They offered a "top notch education" to their young charges. They organized after-school and weekend activities. They opened a mission store to help clothe the needy and taught First Aid and nutrition classes to impoverished young pregnant women. They worked in ecumenical cooperation with local churches.
>
> In short, says Thea, "they made a difference in the lives of my people, my town." They made a fundamental difference in her life as well. Thea converted to Catholicism and entered the convent in the 10th grade. ("A Woman Wrapped in Courage" [Jan. 1989]: 1)

Father Justin, Bertha's pastor, suggested that she join the Holy Family Community of Black Sisters in New Orleans, but she was determined to go to La Crosse. Her father warned her, "They are not going to like you up there, the only black in the middle of all the whites." Bertha's response was, "I'm going to make them like me."

And she did. But she had to get used to a change in food and weather. She slept in a dormitory in a bed enclosed in white curtains and prayed in a formal manner. Bertha Bowman adjusted, learned, and made fast friends.

Sometime in 1955, Bertha developed tuberculosis. She was sent to River Pines Sanatorium in Stevens Point, Wisconsin. Visits from her parents and letters of support and encouragement from her friends in Canton and her mentors and classmates in La Crosse helped Bertha get well in a year's time. The postulants at Saint Rose High School sent her a newspaper regularly. Called Saint Joseph's Journal, it was handwritten in newspaper-column style and "published exclusively for Bertha Bowman."

While at River Pines, Bertha took a correspondence course in English composition from the University of Wisconsin. She entitled one of her essays "Away f'om Home." This essay describes her love and longing for her folks, her town, and her culture. Even though the year was 1955 and she was living in an almost exclusively white environment, Bertha Bowman had enough pride in her black heritage and language to write the essay in a southern black voice. Her instructor must have been culturally sensitive and sensible, because she or he gave Bertha an *A* for the essay.

It seems as if the winter's really heah now—ice an' snow an' cold an' ice an' snow. I ain't complainin', jes I thought you all might like t' know. You all has never seed the trees bent t' the breakin', branches bowed beneath their load. You all has never seed the ole ones pick their way with feet and cane, whilst the young'ons slip an' slide not carin' where they fall. You all has never seed the little birdies fluffin' out their feathers and a tryin' t' keep warm. But it's heah now, and I sorta reckon that the winter's really come t' stay a while.

The grass is all gone, an' the snow is lyin' on the groun' an' the sky is lookin' mighty dark and dreary like stoim was threatnin'. The church bells sound all muffled in the city like somebuddy had been tamperin' wid the very elements, and it's awful cold.

An' when I told theseyere Northern folks that you all said it was 'bout eighty in the shade, they laughed an' asked me what was Christmas widout snow. But I didn't laugh. I jes told them 'bout the rains an' 'bout the gardens, spring an' fall, an' 'bout that dreadful year when we had one whole inch o' snow, an' no one had the fuel, an' the 'lectric power mill broke down, an' we was cold.

Up heah, it's right smart diff'ent though. Everybuddy has his boots an' scarf, an' everybuddy has a big warm coat. Up heah is tol'able. I got me nice warm clothes; so I ain't sufferin' from the cold. Don't you all worry now, 'cause I ain't cold a'tall.

But still, I hates t' see them icy fingers hangin' from the roof 'til some is reachin' nigh t' four feet long. Sho nuff, the very sight o' them jes sets my spine t' shiverin', an' I long t' see them old poinsett'as bloomin' in the yard an' the pretty grass an' flowers. The sleigh bells ringin' fur off in the distance, what fills theseyere folk wid winter cheer, tugs at my po' heart an' fills my soul with sadness. Been so long since I heard the night birds singin'. Been so long since I seed you all.

Then when the meal time comes, it really sets my mouth a waterin' fo' that there chicken Southern fried, an' for some hominy grits or some o' them fluffy, nice, high hoe-cakes like ole Mama cooks. I'd like to see that Yankee what could turn a dish t' suit a Dixie tongue.

Then there's the nights; I lies abed an' dreams that I 'as stranded in the sno', an' I can heah the old folks callin', but I jes can't move along. Sometimes I think as if I'll never git t' see that old bayou no mo'. Sometimes I think as if I'll never make it home.

I ain't complainin', but you all can see that thisyere ain't at all like home. Nossuh! I ain't complainin', but thisyere ain't like home a'tall.

৩ 3 ৩

Learning and Teaching

School was a place to go to enjoy life.

Sister Thea's parents planned for her education from the moment of her birth. She once remarked:

> The day I was born, my father went out and started a separate bank account for my education. As far back as I can remember, education was a top priority in my family on both sides. My mother's mother was a teacher and a school principal. Even today, the school she founded in Greenville, Mississippi, is still named after her. And my father's father was a slave, but he managed to go to school through the second grade. So the expectation was that education was important, not just for yourself but for your family and your community. And it brought responsibility to try to help somebody else. That's a different kind of teaching from what many families believe today.

As a sister in formation, Thea prepared herself for teaching. She earned her Bachelor of Arts degree at Viterbo College in La Crosse, Wisconsin. In 1958, she began teaching grades 5 and 6 at Blessed Sacrament School. Thea's students deeply loved and respected her. One little boy who had gotten into trouble in another Catholic school was transferred to Blessed Sacrament. At the end of the first day in Thea's class, he eased into the social worker's car and said, "Gosh, she's beautiful."

From 1961 to 1968, Sister Thea taught English and vocal music at Holy Child Jesus Catholic High School in her hometown of Canton. Here

Sister Thea gloried in doing some "down-home teaching" and in showing her students what a gift it was to be black and Catholic.

Then Sister Thea's superiors asked her to complete a doctorate so that she could return to Viterbo College and teach English. Sister Thea received her master's degree in 1969 and her doctorate in 1972, both from the Catholic University of America. For her doctoral dissertation, she showed how Saint Thomas More supported "faith by reason and using all the rhetorical tools at his disposal, built his argument for spiritual comfort" for his family and friends whom he was soon to leave by death.

When she finished her doctorate, Sister Thea toured Europe and studied at Oxford University for a summer. Then, in the fall of 1972, she started teaching English at Viterbo and eventually became chair of the department. Students in Sister Thea's writing classes remember her insistence that "you have a right to any idea you can support" and her "cool, maddening, Socratic method of questioning." Knowing their propensity to be wordy, she would simply write, "More Hemingway and less Henry James." Thea expected students to be part of a classroom community, telling them: "Let your light shine. Each one teach one. Walk your talk."

About a year before her death, Sister Thea's remarks about studying and teaching at Viterbo were compiled into an article for *Viterbo Strides*, the alumni magazine. Her comments summarize many of her attitudes about learning and teaching.

ᐤ\ᐤ ᐤ\ᐤ ᐤ\ᐤ

"Viterbo [was] a place where my teachers were very dedicated and they shared their love for learning. I remember Viterbo as a refuge. School was a place to go to enjoy life.

"I remember my classmates going and studying chemistry and physics and some of the more rigorous disciplines. I was an English major with a minor in drama and I was just having fun. I loved literature and I met teachers who were able to help me open up the books, teachers who realized that I had some gift. That was something that had never occurred to me: to realize that I could do things like think, read, write. I remember my English classes and my religion classes. I was in the first Viterbo class that adapted the physical sciences to the needs of

---

Sister Thea's reflections on Viterbo College are reprinted from "A Final Farewell to Sister Thea Bowman," *Viterbo Strides* (Fall 1990): 6–7.

students who were not . . . science majors. So I was in the first class designed for people who needed to know physics for life, or biology just for ordinary living. That was exciting to me. Viterbo College was a good experience for me as a student.

"But it was a lonely experience for me culturally, because very little of what I studied pertained to my past, my experience, the contributions of my people.

"I came back to Viterbo in 1972 as a teacher, full of enthusiasm for Viterbo, for teaching, for learning, and I met some fascinating students who made my life here very, very exciting.

"I used to teach freshmen and I taught what was called survival course: 'How to Get Through College.' I was surprised to find that so many of the students that I met as freshmen were spending most of their time trying to figure out what somebody else wanted them to think and what somebody else wanted them to say. I tried to show them that surviving college was simple. . . .

". . . As a teacher of English and chairman of the English Department, one of my primary objectives was that I should have a good time, that my students should have a good time and enjoy what we were doing. That got me into trouble sometimes. . . .

"Viterbo was small, Viterbo was family. You knew your teachers, you knew your students; and I think as Viterbo grew and expanded, there were people who were dedicated to trying to maintain that kind of family atmosphere. It was expressed in a care and concern for students' intellectual development, for professional development, for human and personal development. And to me, that was what made the difference.

"[Saint] Francis said that all his followers needed were to be minstrels and troubadours going about the countryside, teaching the good news, singing and praising. Somebody like me, a teacher of the English language and literature, was made to be a minstrel and troubadour.

"I think of the Franciscan character in the early days of Viterbo. . . . The students, as well as the faculty, were inspired by the prayer of St. Francis: 'Make me an instrument of your peace.' For as long as I was here, the Franciscan ideal was assumed and expressed.

"There's also a kind of craziness that is Franciscan. And that was part of Viterbo, too. People took time to laugh, time to play and it wasn't an isolated thing. I think about the time when I was here and there was a closeness and kind of love that was Franciscan. Is it still like that?"

Part B
Black Spirituality

4

Being a Black Catholic

We have come a long way in faith. . . . We as black people find ourselves at the threshold of a new age.

In her address to the United States bishops assembled at Seton Hall University on 17 June 1989, Sister Thea asked for empowerment for her people. She called for a church that would be truly catholic, a church in which the gifts of all people of the world would be welcome.

She began by singing "Sometimes I feel like a motherless child / A long way from home," and she asked: "Can you hear me church, will you help me church? I'm a pilgrim in the journey looking for home, and Jesus told me the church is my home, and Jesus told me that heaven is my home and I have here no lasting city. Cardinals, archbishops, bishops: My brothers or church, please help me to get home."

What does it mean to be black in these United States? What does it mean to be an African American?

Sister Thea's address to the bishops is reprinted from "To Be Black and Catholic," *Origins* (6 July 1989): 114–118.

Our History

Our history includes the services of Simon of Cyrene, the search of the Ethiopian eunuch, the contributions of black Egypt in art and mathematics and monasticism and politics, the art and architecture of Zimbabwe, the scholarship of Timbuktu, the dignity and serenity of textile and gold and religion in Ghana, the pervasive spirituality and vitality of Nigeria, the political and social systems of Zaire.

Our history includes enslavements, oppression and exploitation. As Malcolm X said, "My folks, most of them, didn't come over here on the Mayflower; they came over here on slave ships, in chains."

Proud, strong men and women, artists, teachers, healers, warriors and dream makers, inventors and builders, administrators like yourselves, politicians, priests: They came to these shores in the slave trade. Those who survived the indignity of the middle passage came to the American continents bringing treasures of African heritage, African spiritual and cultural gifts, wisdom, faith and faithfulness, art and drama. Here in an alien land; African people clung to African ways of thinking, of perceiving, of understanding values, of celebrating life, of walking and talking and healing and learning and singing and praying.

. . . African ways of laughing and being together and loving: That's culture.

To the Americas our people brought the secret memory of Africa, the celebration of life values in an African way and style: in song and instrumentation, in story and drum, in verse and anecdote, the memory of the survival mechanisms of Africa, the memory of color and texture, of culinary arts that translated even when we ate chitlins and other folks' leftovers.

African people here became African Americans. Expressing faith in the God who loves and saves, they embodied and celebrated their own lives and their own values, their goals, their dreams, their relationships. Our history includes the island experience—the Virgin Islands, Haiti, Cuba; our Hispanic experience in Central and South America; our native experience, where African blood commingled with Choctaw and Chickasaw and Cherokee, with people of Asian and Asian-Pacific origin, with Europeans from France and Germany. You want to know how come some of us look like we do?

African people of the diaspora, we are here in this land, and this is our land. That's part of our history too.

Our people, black people, helped to build this nation in cotton and grain and beans and vegetables, in brick and mortar.

They cleared the land and cooked the food that they grew.

They cleaned houses and built churches, some of them Catholic churches. They built railroads and bridges and national monuments.

Black people defended this country as soldiers and sailors. Black people taught and molded and raised the children—and I'm not just talking about the black children. . . .

You know what I'm talking about, church? I mean, are you walking with me, church?

Surviving our history, physically, mentally, emotionally, morally, spiritually, faithfully and joyfully, our people developed a culture that was African and American, that was formed and enriched by all that we experienced. And despite all this, despite the civil rights movement of the '60s and the socio-educational gains of the '70s, blacks in the '80s are still struggling, still scratching and clawing as the old folks said, still trying to find home in the homeland and home in the church, still struggling to gain access to equal opportunity.

A disproportionate number of black people are poor. Poverty, deprivation, discrimination, stunted physical, intellectual and spiritual growth—I don't need to tell you this, but I want to remind you, more than a third of the black people that live in the United States live in poverty, the kind of poverty that lacks basic necessity.

I'm talking about old people who have worked hard all their lives and don't have money for adequate food or shelter or medical care.

I'm talking about children who can never have equal access and equal opportunity because poverty doomed them to low birth weight and retardation and unequal opportunity for education.

More than 55 percent of black babies are born to single mothers. About 41 percent of black families are single-parent families headed by women. The divorce rate for blacks is twice as high as for whites.

Black children are twice as likely as white children to be born prematurely, to suffer from low birth weight, to live in substandard housing, to have no parent employed.

Unemployment and underemployment among us are endemic. And many of us don't have the social and political contacts that put us where the jobs are when jobs are being passed out. One of every 21 black males is murdered. A disproportionate number of our men are dying of suicide and AIDS and drug abuse and low self-esteem.

Black and Catholic

What does it mean to be black and Catholic? For many of us it means having been evangelized, having been educated, having been given a chance through the work of the Catholic Church, through the Josephites or the Divine Word Fathers or the Holy Ghost Fathers or the Franciscans or the Edmundites or the Sisters of the Blessed Sacrament.

I'm from Mississippi. The first schools in Mississippi were started in the cathedral basement by diocesan priests and a group of lay women. For so many of us, being black and Catholic means having come into the church because education opened the door to evangelization. It means, in an age when black men and black women were systematically kept out of the priesthood and out of most religious communities, there were those who cared and who came and who worked with and for us and among us and helped us to help ourselves.

And now our black American bishops, in the name of the church universal, have publicly declared that we as a people of faith, as a Catholic people of God, have come of age. And it is time for us to be evangelizers of ourselves.

What does it mean to be black and Catholic? It means that I come to my church fully functioning. That doesn't frighten you, does it? I come to my church fully functioning. I bring myself, my black self, all that I am, all that I have, all that I hope to become, I bring my whole history, my traditions, my experience, my culture, my African-American song and dance and gesture and movement and teaching and preaching and healing and responsibility as gift to the church.

I bring a . . . spirituality [that] is contemplative and biblical and holistic, bringing to religion a totality of minds and imagination, of memory, of feeling and passion and emotion and intensity, of faith that is embodied, incarnate praise, . . . a spirituality that is communal, that tries to walk and talk and work and pray and play together—even with the bishops. You know, when our bishop is around, we want him to be where we can find him, where we can reach out and touch him, where we can talk to him. Don't be too busy, you-all.

A spirituality that in the middle of your Mass or in the middle of your sermon just might have to shout out and say, "Amen, hallelujah, thank you Jesus." A faith that attempts to be Spirit-filled. The old ladies say that if you love the Lord your God with your whole heart, [with] your whole soul and your whole mind and all your strength, then you praise the Lord with your whole heart and soul and mind and strength and you don't bring him any feeble service.

If you get enough fully functioning black Catholics in your diocese, they are going to hold up the priest and they are going to hold up the bishop. We love our bishops, you-all. We love you-all too. But see, these bishops are our own, ordained for the church universal, ordained for the service of God's people, but they are ours; we raised them; they came from our community and in a unique way they can speak for us and to us. And that's what the church is talking about. Indigenous leadership. The leaders are supposed to look like their folks, ain't that what the church says?

To be black and Catholic means to realize that the work of the ordained ministers is not a threat to me and I'm no threat to that. The work of the ordained minister, of the professional minister, is to enable the people of God to do the work of the church. To feed us sacramentally, to enable us to preach and to teach, and I ain't necessarily talking about preaching in the pulpit.

You know as well as I do that some of the best preaching does not go on in the pulpit, but as a Catholic Christian I have a responsibility to preach and to teach, to worship and to pray. Black folk can't just come into church and depend on the preacher and say, "Let Father do it." And if Father doesn't do it right, then they walk out and they complain, you know, "That liturgy didn't do anything for me."

The question that we raise is, What did you do for the liturgy? And the church is calling us to be participatory and to be involved. The church is calling us to feed and to clothe and to shelter and to teach. Your job is to enable me, to enable God's people, black people, white people, brown people, all the people, to do the work of the church in the modern world. Teaching, preaching, witnessing, worshiping, serving, healing and reconciling in black, because wedded to the lived experience, to the history and the heritage of black people.

Getting in touch. To be black and Catholic means to get in touch with the world church, with my brothers and sisters in Rome, with my brothers and sisters in China, with my brothers and sisters in Europe and Asia and Latin America, with the church of Africa. Do your folk realize that there are more Catholic Christians in Africa than in North America, and then they run around talking about the minority? In Africa right now 300 people become Christian every day, and 75 percent of them are becoming Roman Catholics.

The Vatican central office reports that in Africa the number of students for the priesthood increased by 88 percent between 1970 and 1988, while in North America the number dropped by 43 percent.

To be black and Catholic means to be intensely aware of the changing complexion of the College of Cardinals. I picked up your Catholic newspaper and I saw the picture church, world church, and a lot of folk look like me. We've got to get the word out. To be black and Catholic still, though, often feels like being a second- or third-class citizen of the holy city.

Black Leadership in the Church

You know, Bishop Jim Lyke said a long time ago that black Catholic Christians will be second-class citizens of the church until they take their places in leadership beside their brothers and sisters of whatever race or national origin. . . .

The majority of priests, religious and lay ministers who serve the black community in the United States still are not from the black community, and many of those people who attempt to serve among us . . . do not feel an obligation to learn or understand black history or spirituality or culture or life, black tradition or ritual. They work for the people, but they have not learned to share life and love and laughter with the people. They somehow insulate themselves from the real lives of the people because they don't feel comfortable with black people.

I travel all over the country, and I see it: black people within the church, black priests, sometimes even black bishops, who are invisible. And when I say that, I mean they are not consulted. They are not included. Sometimes decisions are made that affect the black community for generations, and they are made in rooms by white people behind closed doors.

Some of us are poor. Some of us have not had the advantages of education. But how can people still have a voice and a role in the work of the church? Isn't that what the church is calling us all to?

I see people who are well educated and experienced and willing to work. Sometimes they're religious; sometimes they're lay. They are not included in the initial stages of planning. They are not included in the decision making. Now, I know you are bishops and I'm not talking about somebody coming into your diocese and trying to tell you what to do. I'm talking about the normal, church-authorized consultative processes that attempt to enable the people of God to be about the work of the Catholic Church. If you know what I'm talking about, say Amen.

See, you-all talk about what you have to do if you want to be a multicultural church: Sometimes I do things your way; sometimes you do things mine. . . .

Black people who are still victims within the church of paternalism, of a patronizing attitude, black people who within the church have developed a mission mentality—they don't feel called, they don't feel responsible, they don't do anything. Let Father do it, let the sisters do it, let the friends and benefactors from outside do it. That's the mission mentality. And it kills us and it kills our churches. And so, within the church, how can we work together so that all of us have equal access to input, equal access to opportunity, equal access to participation?

Go into a room and look around and see who's missing and send some of your folks out to call them in so that the church can be what she claims to be, truly catholic.

They still talk about black folk in the church. You hear it, you know, you hear it over on the sidelines. They say we're lazy. They say we're loud. They say we're irresponsible. They say we lower the standards. So often we've been denied the opportunities to learn and to practice. You learned by trial and error; ain't that how you learned? And to grow.

Some black people don't approve of black religious expression in Catholic liturgy. They've been told that it's not properly Catholic. They've been told that it's not appropriately serious or dignified or solemn or controlled, that the European way is necessarily the better way.

How can we teach all the people what it means to be black and Catholic? The *National Catechetical Directory* says that all catechesis is supposed to be multicultural, but how little of it is. When we attempt to bring our black gifts to the church, people who do not know us say we're being non-Catholic or separatists or just plain uncouth.

Catholic Education

I've got to say one more thing. You-all ain't going to like this but that's all right. Catholic schools have been a primary instrument of evangelization within the black community. The church has repeatedly asked black folk, what do you want, what can the church do for you? And black folk all over the country are saying, Help us to education. We need education. The way out of poverty is through education.

We can't be church without education, because ignorance cripples us and kills us. Black people are still asking the Catholic Church for education. Now, sometimes we don't have the money. Are we finding alternative ways to speak to the black community in a language that they understand? Bishop Brunini said a lot of Catholics spend time ministering to the saved and go out there and work with the church folks. A lot of black people out there are unchurched.

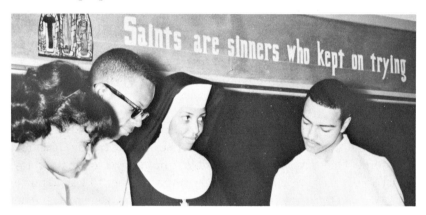

We Shall Overcome

We have come a long way in faith. Just look where we have come from. We as black people find ourselves at the threshold of a new age. And as I look about the room I know that many of you have walked and talked and worked and prayed and stood with us in society and in the church. And in the name of all black folk, I thank you.

Today we're called to walk together in a new way toward that land of promise and to celebrate who we are and whose we are. If we as church walk together, don't let nobody separate you. That's one thing black folk can teach you. Don't let folk divide you or put the lay folk over here and the clergy over here, put the bishops in one room and the clergy in the other room, put the women over here and the men over here.

The church teaches us that the church is a family. It is a family of families and the family got to stay together. We know that if we do stay together, if we walk and talk and work and play and stand together in Jesus' name, we'll be who we say we are, truly Catholic; and we shall overcome—overcome the poverty, overcome the loneliness, overcome the alienation and build together a holy city, a new Jerusalem, a city set apart where they'll know we are his because we love one another.

"We shall overcome" (You all get up!)
"We shall overcome
"We shall overcome
"We shall overcome someday
"Oh, deep in my heart,
"Deep in my heart I know,
"I do believe we shall overcome someday."

Now, bishops I'm going to ask you-all to do something. Cross your right hand over your left hand. You've got to move together to do that. All right now, walk with me. See, in the old days, you had to tighten up so that when the bullets would come, so that when the tear gas would come, so that when the dogs would come, so that when the horses would come, so that when the tanks would come brothers and sisters would not be separated from one another.

And you remember what they did with the clergy and the bishops in those old days, where they'd put them? Right up in front, to lead the people in solidarity with our brothers and sisters in the church who suffer in South Africa, who suffer in Poland, who suffer in Ireland, who suffer in Nicaragua, in Guatemala, in Northern Ireland, all over this world. We shall live in love.

"We shall live in love
"We shall live in love
"We shall live in love today
"Deep in my heart,
"Deep in my heart I know I do believe,
"We shall live in love."

That's all we've got to do: love the Lord, to love our neighbor. Amen. Amen. Amen. Amen.

જ\૭ જ\૭ જ\૭

At the end of her presentation, a bouquet of red roses was presented to Sister Thea. She said: "In the name of all the mothers and grandmothers and aunts and friends, all the women who have brought you to priesthood, who have nurtured you toward episcopacy, who have strengthened you in faith and hope and love so that you can be the church of Jesus Christ, I accept these beautiful roses."

5

Spirituality:
The Soul of the People

> Black American spirituality . . . is at once a response to and a reflection on Black life and culture.

Eager to have people understand the religious experience of African Americans, Sister Thea often spoke and wrote about their spirituality. She delivered this speech at the National Black Sisters' Conference in 1982.

Spirituality is conscious contact with the Spirit that is God, who is above us, who transcends and inspires us. It is conscious contact with the spirit that is "self," with the inner-self where memory, imagination, intellect, feelings and the body are caught up in the search for humanity. Spirituality is conscious contact with the spirit that is community, with the chemistry, the dynamic that bonds us together when we are gathered in peak moments of joy or grief, struggle or aspiration. In a word, Spirituality is at once God-awareness, self-awareness, and other-awareness. It is the level of consciousness and of choosing that makes us different from the pelican that dies on the beach and simply is no more.

"Spirituality: The Soul of the People" is reprinted from *Tell It Like It Is: A Black Catholic Perspective on Christian Education* (Oakland, CA: National Black Sisters' Conference [NBSC], 1983), pp. 84–85.

    Spirituality is faith lived. As such, it encompasses the totality of personal and collective responses to religious belief—relationships, morality, worship, and daily living. As Christians we strive to understand and to act in a way that makes us part of the reality that is the will and purpose of God. We strive to let ourselves feel, remember . . . that which we believe. Spirituality, then, is operative on cognitive, affective and volitional levels: It encompasses the whole person—their mind, heart and will.

Black American Spirituality . . . is at once a response to and a reflection on Black life and culture. It is rooted in our African heritage, with its ways of perceiving and valuing reality, its style of expression, its modes of prayer and contemplating the divine. It is colored by our Middle Passage, Slavery, our Island and Latin experience, segregation, integration, and our on-going struggle for liberation. It is manifest in diverse life-styles: Single, married and celibate. It is expressed in every geographic locale whether urban or rural, southern, northern, eastern or western. It is present in every socio-economic level: Rich, middle-class, and poor. Our Spirituality is influenced by our own experiences and that of our peers and forebears in Pentecostal, Baptist, Adventist, Episcopal, Methodist, Catholic and other churches, making it bear elements of high church, low church, grass-roots, down-home-cotton-patch and no institutional church at all. It is shaped by our self-description as Black, Negro, Creole or Colored. Regardless of the circumstance, wherever Blacks have sought to find meaning, purpose, identity, community, worth, and God-together, Black Spirituality has grown and flourished.

Black Spirituality is characterized by:

a contemplative approach to prayer; a sense of God's power and presence everywhere; a high value placed on emotional response; a fundamental rejection of any 'body-is-evil' spirituality; a sense that joy is the important spiritual good; an awareness of the social justice dimensions of religion; and finally, a sense that Blacks are as a people a spiritual people—that we have a heritage to pass on. (Cyprian Davis, "The Black Contribution to a North American Spirituality," *New Catholic World* 225 [July–Aug. 1982]: 184)

While speaking of *a* Black Spirituality it must be understood that Blacks are not all alike. The emphasis and expression of our Spirituality, therefore, is not all alike. There are uniquenesses within the collective. There are diverse preferences within our corporate spirituality. It is important to understand the collective reality, but this reality cannot be known in isolation from its constituent parts. . . . In terms of Black Spirituality, the question becomes "How can we know, participate in, and impact the encounter with God, the mode and view of life of the Black people who make up my community?"

The answer to that question will only come if we can hear, see and be touched by the people. By constructing a framework for active listening, we can begin to grasp that magnitude of the oral and aural tradition which is the most eloquent expression of Black Spirituality.

Part C
Music and Black Spirituality

6

The Sound of Black Spirituality

Black music is a living repository of the thoughts, feelings and will of Black Spirituality. Its symbols, images, rhythms and expressed values take Blacks *home*.

Sister Thea once remarked, "Our songs articulate the root and essence of Black spirituality." She spoke and wrote extensively on the message of black music. In the introduction to her book *Sister Thea: Songs of My People* (Boston: St. Paul Books and Media, 1989), Thea explained how music became part of the fabric of her life and her spirituality:

When I was a child in Canton, Mississippi, my people sang the songs of faith—songs of Adam and Eve, Cain and Abel, Noah, Moses, David, and Jesus. The songs of faith were passed on, taught, learned, and prayed in an environment of love and celebration. I learned them from Mama, who sang me to sleep, who sang for me and with me in so many special and well-remembered moments; from Mother Rica who gathered twenty-five or thirty children around her in her warm home and sang faith songs that called forth energy and enthusiasm, that invited bodily response, that were fun; from Mrs. Ward, our next-door neighbor, who sang as she worked her garden or hung out wash and fed her chickens, who hummed as she walked down the street; from other children who sang as they played church and baptism and funeral, or as they sang for simple entertainment and joy; from Sayde and Earnest Garrett and the other Garrett brothers who gathered around our piano and sang with us for hours whenever they came to visit; from all the church folks who sang, played instruments, and danced, or who in their faces and bodies reflected the power and beauty of the songs of faith. Sharing the songs of faith bonded us in family and church. Sharing the songs brought hope and consolation and joy.

I did not realize I was receiving a religious education—that I was being taught prayer, salvation history, morals and values, faith, hope, love, and joy. I did not realize that the songs would form the basis of my lifelong religious education and the catalyst that would impel me to seek books and classes, exegesis and explication de texte in my eagerness to know and understand more of the Words of Salvation. I did not know that I was being taught modes of prayer that would increasingly enrich my personal prayer, community prayer, liturgical prayer; modes of prayer that I have been privileged to share with my brothers, sisters, and children of diverse races and culture, economic backgrounds, and religions.

I did not realize that the songs would bring to me and to those I love comfort in sorrow, solace in grief, refuge in time of trouble, relief even from physical pain—always strength and hope, peace and joy. (P. 3)

When Thea taught in her hometown, she formed a fifty-voice choir called the Holy Child Jesus Singers. They made an album, *The Voice of Negro America,* that was "dedicated to the promotion of brotherhood and universal peace." Between songs on the recording, Sister Thea said:

Listen! Hear us! While the world is full of hate, strife, vengeance, we sing songs of love, laughter, worship, wisdom, justice, and peace because we are free. Though our forefathers bent to bear the heat of the sun, the strike of the lash, the chain of slavery, we are free. No man can enslave us. We are too strong, too unafraid. America needs our strength, our voices to drown out her sorrows, the clatter of war. . . . Listen! Hear us! We are the voice of negro America.

At Catholic University, Thea began studying black music as a way of preserving black culture. Soon other universities asked her to speak and sing for them. Back at Viterbo, she formed the Hallelujah Singers. This group performed an extensive repertoire of black music at schools and colleges in the Midwest. And when Thea traveled around the country speaking, even at the end of her life, songs were a substantial part of her dynamic presentations.

In 1982, Sister Thea told the National Black Sisters' Conference about the relationship between black music and black spirituality:

All of the sounds of a people comprise their oral tradition. "Ebonics" (Black sounds) are expressed in conversations, song, stories, jokes, adages, prayers, sermons, poems, street jargon, folk sayings, slang, drama, anecdotes, moans, groans, shouts, hollers and suprasegmental phonemes (i.e., "yes," "well," "Lord, Lord," and "Amen"). Some defy precise interpretation, but all precisely express the Black experience. Black sounds lift up for our hearing Black God-awareness, self-awareness and other-awareness. . . .

Black music is a living repository of the thoughts, feelings and will of Black Spirituality. Its symbols, images, rhythms and expressed values take Blacks *home:* Back to mamas and daddys, grandparents, godparents, aunts, uncles, neighbors and friends who taught us to "hold on" in faith, hope and love. Black music lifts up the lives we lived and live. Blacks preserve their music with care and consciously pass it on as it makes present their significant events, heroes, heroines, values, struggles, and ambitions. It has multi-level appeal—engaging the whole person. The ageless appeal of the themes—the fact that Blacks have treasured and shared them in every generation—is a clear indication that they nourish, inspire, revitalize and resonate with the heart of Black Spirituality. They provide us with a valuable resource for catechesis and for knowing those to be catechized.

Traveling across the country, I hear young and old sharing Black music. Children, youths, and adults know the old songs. They adapt the old melodies to their own new rhythms and harmonies. They adapt the old words, themes and insights to their present situation. Arrangements by Roderick Bell, James Cleveland, Clarence Rivers, Andre Crouch, Ron Harbor, Edwin Hawkins, Roger Holliman, Robert Ray, Grayson Brown and others can be heard in small churches, in the chapels of academic institutions, in cathedrals, in homes and at celebrations of every description. Wherever, whenever, with whomever Blacks need to re-create their mind, disposition and spirit, they sing, play and participate in their music. It is lyrical and rhythmic expressions of faith, identity and relatedness.

The excerpts from Sister Thea's presentation to the 1982 NBSC are reprinted from "Spirituality: The Soul of My People," pp. 3, 85, 87–92.

The God-Awareness

Black music reveals God as Protector, Creator, Sustainer of Life, Great Freedom-Fighter, Liberator, the Ultimate Source of Strength. The recurring affirmation is GOD IS.

> God is my father and my mother.
> He's my sister and my brother.
> He is my rock, my sword, my shield.
> He's a wheel within the middle of a wheel.
> He is water when you're thirsty and
> Bread when you're hungry.
>
> He's a father to the fatherless,
> He's a mother to the motherless.
> He's a joy when you're in sorrow.
> He's your hope for tomorrow.
>
> He's my life. He's my everything.
> He's my doctor, He's my lawyer, He's mine indeed.
> He's everything I need.

Black music speaks of God's creative love, infinite fidelity, vigilant protection and eminent justice in a wealth of songs about Adam and Eve, Methusela, Noah, Abraham, Isaac, Jacob, Moses, the Exodus, Joshua, the wilderness, Saul, David, Elijah, Ezekiel, Daniel, Shadrach, Meshach, Abendego, Daniel in the lion's den, and countless others. The themes are not chosen happpenstance. They are deliberate choices as their composers are deliberately bringing the values of the scripture to bear on the current reality. The songs are sung with imagery that makes them come to life. Our music is an experience that marshalls the forces of the body to become part of it. Biblical history then becomes our history. The personages become our ancestors. The events become our reality. The response called for by the values expressed becomes our responsibility and expectation. The agony and the triumph becomes our own.

> Po' little Jesus
> Him born on Christmas
> Him born on Friday.
> Didn't have no cradle.
> Didn't have no hotel room. . . .

Our music speaks of the personal implications for us of the Christ-event: The wonder of it, the power of it, our giftedness by it. . . .

> Dey crucified my Lord,
>> An' He never said a mumblin' word.
> Dey nailed Him to a tree,
>> An' He never said a mumblin' word.
> Dey pierced Him in de side,
> De blood cam trinklin' down,
> He bowed His head an' died,
>> An' He never said a mumblin' word.

Self-Awareness

The perception of Jesus as Brother-Savior and of the Father-God's enduring protective love provide the basis for our assurance: We may be sinners, but we are redeemed; we may be rejected by others, but we are children of God; we may be oppressed for a while, but God keeps his promises—so "trouble don't last always." Like all other people, Blacks need a sense of wholeness, worth, esteem, trust, and autonomy. Our music, old and new, leads us to seek strength and security in the fidelity of the Lord. It records and celebrates an optimistic stance and attitude toward life. Our cares, concerns, pains and frustrations are brought with confidence to the Lord in our acknowledgment that we need and expect to receive God's help.

> Sometimes I'm up, sometimes I'm down,
>> But still my soul is glory-bound. . . .

Other-Awareness

Out of the expressed Black American Christian understanding of God and self, arises a predictable understanding and attitude of our relationship to others: We are called to be family in our homes, our communities, our churches, and in the Kingdom of God.

> Let us break bread together,
> Let us drink wine together,
> Let us praise God together,
>> on our knees. . . .

Our music verbalizes the continual appeal *from* the community, *by* the community, to conversion, commitment, and *to* community:

> Sinner, sinner, you better pray,
> Looks like my Lord a-coming in de sky.
> Or your soul be lost on the judgment day.

> Sinner, please don't let this harvest pass;
> And die and lose your soul at last.

> If there's anybody here like weeping Mary,
> Call upon your Jesus, an' He'll draw near.

> Rise and shine and give God the glory, glory.
> Come on, mourners, and get ready, ready.
> Come on, children, and don't be weary, weary.
>   For de year of Jubilee.

Our spirituality disposes us to collective responsibility and sharing of resources. Our music identifies our communal needs and bears witness to our communal belief that the Word of God is Good News:

> Good News! The chariot's a-coming

> Go tell it on the mountain
> Over the hills and everywhere,
> Go tell it on the mountain,
> That Jesus Christ is born.

The heavenly community so often referred to in Black music articulates our belief that a day will come when the forces that divide us will be no more. On that day all will acknowledge the reign of God, all will be equal sharers in one community, all will be reunited as family in a home purchased by the love of God. Mindful that Blacks do not dichotomize sacred and secular, heaven is both a temporal hope and a time to come. Blacks are at once expressing their belief that heaven will come in the next life and that heaven is possible for us now if we would live as the Lord asks.

> I'm gonna sit at the welcome table.
> I'm gonna drink from the golden fountain.
> I'm gonna talk with my sisters and brothers.
> We're gonna meet with our King Jesus one of these days.

7

Songs of My People

Each spiritual is in its own way a prayer—of yearning or celebration, of praise, petition, or contemplation, a simple lifting of heart, mind, voice, and life to God.

The songs that Thea selected for *Sister Thea: Songs of My People* and her reflections on them form a rich mine of information about Thea and about black spirituals. At the beginning of the book, Sister Thea gave specific directives for praying the Scriptures with the spirituals and for teaching the Bible through spirituals.

Praying the Scripture with Spirituals

Each spiritual is in its own way a prayer—of yearning or celebration, of praise, petition, or contemplation, a simple lifting of heart, mind, voice, and life to God.

1. Choose a place of quiet and reflection. Shut out distractions.
2. Gently move with the music. Let it calm your body. Let yourself become engaged, participatory, involved. Make a conscious effort to work your way into a mode or prayer that combines thought, memory, imagination, and bodily response, that demands action in the real world of every day.
3. Concentrate on the words of the song and the Scriptural images they invoke. Concentrate your energies. Engage your mind, your Biblical memory, your memory of your own experiences of life and of God.

Engage your imagination. See and hear and feel, taste and touch the Biblical reality. See it all in living color. Let the words and music speak to your whole soul, to your feelings, passions, and emotions. Feel what it means to have walked dry-shod through the Reed Sea, to have placed your firstborn child in a manger, to have sat with Jesus by a well of Samaria, to have watched Jesus nailed upon a cross.

4. Pray with the song. Feel God's presence. Contemplate his goodness. Celebrate the Biblical theme in relationship to the daily mystery of God's working in your own life. Celebrate your own faith and hope and love. Pray in your own way. Move peacefully and gently as you feel drawn to discursive meditation or affective prayer or the contemplative prayer of simple resting in union with God.

5. Pray the spirituals from time to time with family or friends. Pray the spirituals from time to time in liturgy. (Pp. 6–7)

Teaching the Scripture with Spirituals

I grew up in a community where the teaching of religion was a treasured role of the elders—grandparents, old uncles and aunts, but also parents, big brothers and sisters, family friends, and church members. Many of the best teachers were not formally educated. But they knew Scripture, and they believed the Living Word must be celebrated and shared. They did not struggle to ask, "Did this Biblical event occur? When or how did it happen?" Somehow they intuited that the stories were concerned with truth more than with factuality. They asked only, "What does this story mean? What did it mean in Biblical times? What does it mean in our lives today? What does it call me to do?"

Their teachings were simple. Their teachings were sound. Their methodologies were such that without effort, I remember their teachings today: songs of Adam, Eve, Noah, Abraham, Moses, Joshua, Miriam, David, Dives, Ezekiel, Daniel, Jonah, John, Mary, Jesus, his birth, his life, his teachings, his miracles, his disciples, his passion, his glory, his promise to us all of eternal life. As I age I continue to grow in understanding of the lessons based upon the songs of faith.

The methodologies were as modern as today's. Teaching the songs of faith required definite cognitive, affective, and behavioral objectives; use of right and left brain teaching-learning techniques; participatory learning; reality-based learning; value learning; multi-sensory appeal; involvement of intellect, memory, imagination, will, and body. The methodologies are simple and engaging. Often they are fun. I hope you'll enjoy trying them.

1. Use the song as background for the prayer of the day.
2. Listen to the song.
3. Sing the song.
4. Tell or read the Bible story.
5. Talk about the story. Talk about its Biblical meaning. Use the best available of exegesis. Use your full knowledge of Biblical history and interpretation, but translate it into the language and idiom of those who have come to share the Word. Talk *with* your students about its meaning in their lives today and now.
6. Depending on their age and preference, lead your students in re-telling or dramatizing or drawing a favorite scene from the story.
7. Again listen to the song.
8. Use the song as prayer with movement or gesture. Provide opportunity for shared prayer.
9. Remind your students to hum, sing, or pray the song as they work or walk or drive. Remind them to share the song with family, friends, and church. Remind them to teach the story of faith to someone that they love. (P. 7)

Dem Bones

The Lord he thought he'd make a man.
Dem bones gonna rise again.
He'd make him out of mud and sand.
Dem bones gonna rise again.

God created Adam and Eve. He made them well. He made them good. But Adam and Eve sinned. They disobeyed. They broke the bond of faith and faithfulness. They brought sin and disorder into this world. God put them out of paradise. But God did not abandon them. Exiled from their true home they had to work out their salvation. But for them and for their descendants there was ever hope of redemption and resurrection.

"Dem bones gonna rise again!" (P. 13)

Deep River

Deep river, my home is over Jordan,
Deep river, Lord, I want to cross over into campground.

Cast out of paradise, exiled and troubled, humanity longed for *home.*

Brought out of Egypt, wandering through desert and wilderness, God's people longed for *home,* the Promised Land across Jordan that would flow with milk and honey.

In the days of slavery, separated from kin and country, my ancestors longed for *home.*

Home is where love is, where you are nurtured and sheltered and challenged and comforted. *Home* is where you are fed and where tears are wiped away, where you find security, where you know you belong.

For slaves who longed so passionately for home, *home* became a figure of heaven, the heavenly City, where there would be no separation, no death, no auction block, no moaning, no weeping or wailing, no sorrow, no loss. The big extended-family, after-harvest gathering at campground, where loved ones who lived and worked apart could pray and sing and walk and talk and eat and laugh and cry together became a figure of the New Jerusalem, the Holy City where all will know we are His because we love one another. (P. 36)

Jonah

Who did swallow Jonah up?
The whale did swallow Jonah up.
Jonah in the belly whole.

The old folks never wondered if Jonah was real or if the whale was real. They knew the Jonah story was eternal *truth*

- *truth* that no man or woman or little child can hide from the power of an all-seeing, all-knowing, all-powerful God,
  "You can run, but you can't hide."
- *truth* that God will save and deliver,
  "Didn't my Lord deliver Jonah from the belly of the whale?"
- *truth* that happiness is found only in following God's all-perfect will,
  "In God's Will is our peace."

Jonah tried to run away from God, but God did not abandon him. The Jonah story reminds us that God will not forsake us and that God is able to work his Holy Will.

Our God is still in the business of saving. He calls you as he called Jonah to speak the prophetic word. What is God asking of you today? Where is God sending you today? In what ways have you tried to escape his Will? (P. 23)

Lord, teach me to listen to your Word.
Lord, send me where you would have me go.
Lord, help me to do your holy will.

                                        (P. 23)

Go Down Moses

Go down, Moses, way down in Egypt's lan',
Tell ol' Pharaoh to let my people go.

In exile and slavery the Israelites called upon the Lord, and in his mercy he delivered them.

God called Moses from among the people to lead the people from slavery and exile into freedom and toward home. As God called Moses, God calls us in his name and by his power to free his people.

My grandpa said the worst slavery is not that which comes from the outside and binds you with ropes or chains. The worst slavery is the slavery that comes in your own heart or in your own home, the slavery to whatever keeps you from being the best that you can be and doing the best that you can do. If we want to free our people, we must daily choose for ourselves the freedom of the sons and daughters of God. (P. 27)

Joshua Fit de Battle of Jericho

> Joshua fit de battle of Jericho,
> An' de walls come tumblin' down.

There were no weapons, no M–16's, no bombs. There was no need for violence. The battle was in God's hands.

God commanded Joshua and the people with the Ark of his Covenanted Presence to encircle Jericho with music, ritual and celebration. God commanded Joshua, and Joshua commanded the people to shout—one Lord, one faith, one united people—and the wall came tumbling down. The power of God and the power of a united, believing people prevailed.

When God is on our side, when we walk in faith and hope and love, no wall, no obstacle can stop us. (P. 40)

> Help us to walk in unity.
>
> . . . .
>
> Help us to overcome selfishness,
>   anger and violence in our hearts,
>   our homes, our Church, our world.
> Help us to knock down, pull down,
>   shout down the walls of racism,
>   sexism, classism, materialism,
>   and militarism that divide and
>   separate us.
> Help us to live as your united people,
>   proclaiming with one voice,
>   our faith, our hope,
>   our love, our joy.
>
>   (P. 40)

Po' Li'l Jesus

> Po' li'l Jesus, born on Christmas,
> Laid in a manger, O my Lawd.
> Po' li'l Jesus, taken from his mothe',
> Nailed to a cross, O my Lawd.

Poor little Jesus, born poor, born rejected, born far away from home.

"Mary's Baby didn't have no cradle. Didn't have no hotel room."

And even at his birth, loomed large the Shadow of the cross.

He came to save the poor and lowly. He, in his flesh, has borne our sorrow. He became like us in all things but sin.

The song is a slave lullaby. Pray it with all the mothers of the world who suffer poverty, neglect, rejection, frustration, violence and oppression. Pray it as you uncover your own poverty.

Thank you, Lord, for in your birth, your life, your death, we find our hope and our joy. (P. 49)

De Blin' Man Stood on de Road an' Cried

> O de blin' man stood on de road an' cried.
> Cryin', 'O my Lord, save-a me.'

The blind man had heard, as we all have heard, that Jesus was a wonder-worker, that Jesus was a healer. And so he joined the crowd in faith to wait for his own miracle. When he heard that Jesus was near, he began to cry out, "Jesus, Son of David, have mercy on me. Jesus, Son of David, have mercy on me. Jesus, Son of David, have mercy on me." (P. 52)

The blind man wanted to see, so he called out to the source of light and sight. His friends told him to shut up, to meld with the crowd, to conform to convention. But the blind man knew how to pray.

Sometimes prayer seems difficult.

Sometimes we think we don't know how to pray. Let us just cry out to Jesus, "Jesus, Son of David, have mercy on me."

> In solitude, "Jesus, Son of David, have mercy on me."
> In our homes and with our families, "Jesus, Son of David, have
>   mercy on me."
> In our churches, "Jesus, Son of David, have mercy on me."

Give me sight. Help me to see your will for me. Help me to see the real needs of my family. Help me to see you in all those I meet. Help me to see you in the oppressed and poor.

Like the blind man, may I see and give you praise.
Like the blind man, may I give thanks and follow you.

(P. 52)

Jesus Met the Woman at the Well

Jesus met the woman at the well,
And he told her everything she had done.

One day Jesus was going from Galilee to Jerusalem. Many Jews used to avoid Samaria like many Blacks used to avoid Mississippi, go miles around just to keep from passing through.

It was not by chance that Jesus stopped at a town in Samaria named Sychar and paused by the cooling, cleansing, refreshing water. He was tired. He was thirsty. He was hungry. He was human. His body needed rest. But he had work to do. It was not by chance that a teacher, a Jewish rabbi without reproach, requested and accepted the ministry of a Samaritan, a stranger, a sinner, a woman.

The well was deep, and he had no bucket. Jews did not ordinarily talk with Samaritans. Rabbis did not ordinarily speak with women in public. Holy people did not ordinarily consort with public sinners. But Jesus said to her, "Give me to drink." He asked her for a favor. He engaged her in conversation. He helped her to identify her own weakness and her strength. She gave him water from the well that was her Samaria. He, in return, gave her water that became in her a spring of living water giving eternal life. She gave him herself as she was, without subterfuge or guile. He healed her guilt and restored her vitality. He transformed her and used her to bring all of Samaria to his feet.

When I acknowledge myself—my true self—weak, failing, incomplete, inconsequential, yet gifted and capable of transcendence; when I accept my neediness and come just as I am, I too can recognize the Messiah, and with joy I shall go running to *my* city crying, "Come! Come! Come, see a Man who told me everything I have done!" (P. 57)

Were You There?

Were you there when they crucified my Lord?
Were you there when they nailed him to the tree?

Were you there when they crucified my Lord? The elders said you had to be there—with mind and heart, with memory and imagination, with feelings and emotions—"to *see* how they done po' Jesus for our sake."

Close your eyes and see Jesus led to Calvary, nailed to the cross. Feel his thirst, his agony, his mother's pain. Hear the torment from the crowd.

Smell the sweat, the blood. Taste the vinegar. Touch the wood of the cross. Watch the Savior's death in all its horror. See him die for you and me. (P. 72)

"For God so loved the world
    that he gave his only begotten Son
so that whosoever believes in him
    would not perish,
but would have everlasting life." (cf. Jn 3:16)
(P. 72)

Go Where I Send Thee

Children, go where I send thee.
How shall I send thee?
I'm gonna send thee one by one.
One for the little bitty baby
Born, born, born in Bethlehem.

"Go into all the world and preach the gospel to the whole creation." (Mk 16:15)

"Go therefore and make disciples of all nations, baptizing them in the name of the Father and of the Son and of the Holy Spirit, teaching them to observe all that I have commanded you; and lo, I am with you always, to the close of the age." (Mt. 28:19–20)

Children, Mothers, Fathers, Sisters, Brothers, go!
There is a song that will never be sung
    unless you sing it.
There is a story that will never be told
    unless you tell it.
There is a joy that will never be shared
    unless you bear it.

    Go tell the world
    Go preach the Gospel
    Go teach the Good News.

        God is. God is love.
        God is with us.
        God is in our lives.

(P. 89)

8

African American Music: Spiritual Power

Black sacred song is designed to move. It moves because depth of feeling gives it "spiritual power."

In 1987, Sister Thea wrote "The Gift of African American Sacred Song"[1] as the introduction to *Lead Me, Guide Me: The African American Catholic Hymnal*. The scholarly essay tells the story of African American sacred song and is a powerful plea for a place within the Catholic church for black sacred music.

From the African Mother Continent, African men and women, through the Middle Passage, throughout the Diaspora, to the Americas, carried the African gift and treasure of sacred song. To the Americas, African men and women brought sacred songs and chants that reminded them of their homelands and that sustained them in separation and in captivity, songs to respond to all life situations, and the ability to create new songs to answer new needs.

African Americans in sacred song preserved the memory of African religious rites and symbols, of a holistic African spirituality, of

---

"The Gift of African American Sacred Song" is reprinted from *Lead Me, Guide Me: The African American Catholic Hymnal* (Chicago: G.I.A. Publications, 1987).

rhythms and tones and harmonies that communicated their deepest feelings across barriers of region and language.

African Americans in fields and quarters, at work, in secret meetings,[2] in slave festivals,[3] in churches, camp meets and revivals, wherever they met or congregated, consoled and strengthened themselves and one another with sacred song—moans, chants, shouts, psalms, hymns, and jubilees, first African songs, then African American songs. In the crucible of separation and suffering, African American sacred song was formed.

In *My Bondage and My Freedom,* Frederick Douglass wrote:

Slaves are generally expected to sing as well as to work. A silent slave is not liked by masters or overseers. 'Make a noise,' 'make a noise,' and 'bear a hand,' are words usually addressed to the slaves when there is silence amongst them. This may account for the almost constant singing heard in the southern states. There was, generally, more or less singing among the teamsters, as it was one means of letting the overseer know where they were, and that they were moving on with the work. But, on allowance day, those who visited the great house farm were peculiarly excited and noisy. While on their way, they would make the dense old woods, for miles around, reverberate with their wild notes. These were not always merry because they were wild. On the contrary, they were mostly of a plaintive cast and told a tale of grief and sorrow. In the most boisterous outbursts of rapturous sentiment, there was ever a tinge of deep melancholy.[4]

As early as 1691, slaves in colonial homes, slave galleries or separate pews participated in worship services with white slave holders. They learned to sing the traditional European psalms and hymns from the *Cambridge Short Tune,* the *Dutch Tune* or the *Hymns and Psalms* of Dr. Watt, which they loved and adapted to their own style and use.[5] In 1755, Reverend Samuel Davies wrote:

The Negroes . . . have an Ear for Musick, and a kind of ecstatic Delight in Psalmody and there are no Books they learn so soon or take so much pleasure in, as those used in the heavenly Part of divine Worship.[6]

Slave records dating back as far as 1723 show there were proficient slave musicians—singers and instrumentalists who played fiddle, vio-

lin, trumpet, drums, guitar, French horn or flute, slave musicians high-
ly valued for their musicianship, slave musicians, some who were able to
read and write.[7]

In 1801, Richard Allen, founder of the African Methodist Episcopal Church, published *A Collection of Hymns and Scriptural Songs from
Various Authors,*[8] hymns and songs which were used by slaves and fugi-
tive slaves in worship. In 1871, the Fisk Jubilee Singers began concert
tours of America and Europe, which for the first time brought the orig-
inal sacred song of Black America to white audiences and to the concert
stage. Harry Burleigh, John Wesley Work, James Weldon and J. Rosa-
mond Johnson scored and arranged Black American sacred songs for
soloists and ensembles in concert performance. In 1921, Thomas A.
Dorsey, the Father of Gospel Music, composed "If I Don't Get There,"
and initiated a new rhythm, a new harmony and a new style. Gospel
singers like Kenneth Morris, Roberta Martin, Mahalia Jackson, James
Cleveland and Edwin Hawkins enriched Black sacred song.

In the sixties, Father Clarence Joseph Rivers revitalized Catholic
worship, inaugurated a revolution in liturgical music, stirred international interest in the indigenization of Catholic Liturgy, and brought
new hope, joy, and spirit to millions of Black Americans when he introduced the melodies, rhythms, harmonies, symbols and rituals of African
American Sacred Song into Roman Catholic worship. His *American
Mass Program* and subsequent compositions and recordings popularized
Black music for Catholic worship. His *Soulfull Worship* and *The Spirit in
Worship* [9] analyzed the history, theology, theory and practice of Black
sacred song and its appropriateness and effectiveness in Catholic litur-
gy and worship.[10] Rawn Harbor, Grayson Brown, Eddie Bonnemere,
Leon Roberts, and others began to compose for Catholic worship.

Black sacred song is soulful song—
1. *holisitic:* challenging the full engagement of mind, imagination,
   memory, feeling, emotion, voice, and body;
2. *participatory:* inviting the worshipping community to join in contemplation, in celebration and in prayer;
3. *real:* celebrating the immediate concrete reality of the worshipping
   community—grief or separation, struggle or oppression, determination or joy—bringing that reality to prayer within the community of believers;
4. *spirit-filled:* energetic, engrossing, intense;
5. *life-giving:* refreshing, encouraging, consoling, invigorating, sustaining.

Influenced by Africa, the Middle Passages, the Islands, Europe and the Americas; created, shaped, treasured, and shared by Black American Christians across time, geographic, socioeconomic and denominational lines, our heritage of sacred song encompasses a vast variety of kinds, styles, and forms.

Wyatt Tee Walker charts the development of five distinctive kinds of Black Sacred Music:[11]

TIME BAR
Black Sacred Music
Period of Development and Dominance

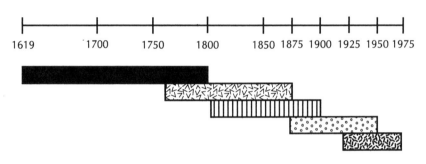

Slave Utterances: moans, chants, cries for deliverance
Spirituals: faith-songs, sorrow songs, plantation hymns, etc.
Meter Music: Watts, Wesley, Sankey, and others
Hymns of Improvisation: Euro-American hymns with "beat"
Gospel Music: music of hard times
(cross-fertilization with secular)

Black sacred song celebrates our God, His goodness, His promise, our faith and hope, our journey toward the promise. Black sacred song carries melodies and tonalities, rhythms and harmonies; metaphors, symbols and stories of faith that speak to our hearts; words, phrases and images that touch and move us.[12]

Stephen Henderson says of Black speech:

Certain words and constructions seem to carry an inordinate charge of emotional and psychological weight, so whenever they are used they set all kinds of bells ringing, all kinds of synapses snapping, on all kinds of levels. . . . I am speaking of words . . . which have levels of meaning that seem to go back to our earliest grappling with the English language in a strange and hostile land. These words, of course, are used in complex associations, and thus form meaningful wholes in ways which defy understanding by outsiders. I call such words "mascon" words, borrowing from (of all places!) the National Aeronautics and Space Administration. NASA invented the acronym to mean "massive concentration" of matter below the lunar surface after it was observed that the gravitational pull on a satellite was stronger in some places than in others.

I use it to mean a massive concentration of Black experimental energy which powerfully affects the meaning of Black speech, Black song, and Black poetry if one, indeed, has to make distinctions.[13]

Black sacred music lifts up Biblical symbols which bear the accumulated meanings of four hundred years of experience of the Black community in America:

> God is Father, Mother, Sister, Brother, Captain,
>   King, Liberator, Friend;
> God is a God of Peace, a God of War;
> God is water to the thirsty, bread to the hungry,
>   shelter to the homeless;
> God is my rock, my sword, my shield;
> God is rest in a weary land;
> God is my all and all.

African people are diunital people, seeking richness of meaning in *apparent* contradiction. They are comfortable with bringing together realities which may appear contradictory or in opposition: for example, body/spirit, sacred/secular, individual/community. They reach toward unification or synthesis of opposites. God is like father and mother (Father—mother—sister—brother symbols are not sexist). God is like fire and balm. African people are comfortable with symbol. African Americans for 400 years have used symbol and song to express a faith and yearning too high, too low, too wide, too deep for words, too passionate to be confined by concepts. As Father Rivers writes:

> Music is important for worship because in worship we have to express the unexpressable, the transcendent, human values that defy ordinary expression. Music, like its other self, poetry, seems capable of doing what plain rational words cannot do: namely, to express the unexpressable, to touch men's hearts, to penetrate their souls, create an experience of things that cannot be reasoned.[14]

Black sacred song—old or new, folk or composed, rural or urban, traditional or contemporary—is in a very real sense, the song *of the people.*
- The music comes from a people who share and claim a common history, common experience, common oppression, common values, hopes, dreams and visions.
- The singer, the singers, the instrumentalists voice the experience and faith of the community.
- The leader (some would say soloist) leads the community in worship. The leader revives and inspirits.

- The worshipping community is active, not passive. People participate—sing, pray, clap, sway, raise their hands, nod their heads. Eye contact, voiced response, the silent testimony of tears, a smile of relief or contemplation or ecstasy says, "This is my story; this is my song."
- The singer is chosen from the people by the people to suit their immediate need.

> "Sometimes *I* feel like a motherless child."
> "*I* just came from the fountain."
> "*I* love the Lord."
> "*My* Heavenly Father watches over *me*."

- The first person pronoun, the 'I' reference is communal. The individual sings the soul of the community. In heart and voice and gesture the Church, the community responds.
- The singer lifts the Church, the people, to a higher level of understanding, feeling, motivation, and participation.

Among African peoples, most art is designed for use, that is to express a feeling or insight, to have an impact in the real world.[15] Song is not an object to be admired so much as an instrument to teach, comfort, inspire, persuade, convince, and motivate. Music is chosen precisely for its effect upon the worshipping community. The aim is *effective* worship. Black sacred song is designed to move. It moves because depth of feeling gives it "spiritual power." Father Clarence Rivers explains:

> A singer who performs without feeling lacks soul. As in original Biblical concept of the spiritual, the spirit or the soul is the life principal, the source of life and liveliness, of dynamism and movement, of motion and emotion. That which is unmoved and unmoving is not spiritual, it is dead! To be spiritual is to be alive, to be capable of moving and responding to movement. . . . Since the Spirit moves, that which does not move would seem to lack the presence of the Spirit.[16]

Black sacred song has been at once a source and an expression of Black faith, spirituality and devotion. By song, our people have called the Spirit into our hearts, homes, churches, and communities. Seeking to enrich our liturgies and lives with the gift of sacred song, we pray:

"Spirit, Sweet Holy Spirit, fall afresh on me."

"Everytime I hear the Spirit
Moving in my heart
I will pray."

Notes

1. Confer Pope Paul IV, "To the Heart of African," *The Pope Speaks* 14, no. 3 (1969): 218–219. This citation concerning cultural pluralism within the Church gives the theological foundation for this essay. Similarly, Pope John Paul II has written numerous commentaries on the place of cultural expression in the Catholic Church.

2. See Miles Mark Fisher, *Negro Slave Songs in the United States* (New York: Citadel Press, 1969), pp. 32–33, 66–79.

3. Festivals in which slaves in large numbers sang in their own African languages survived in the English colonies. Africans gathered to share stories, dances, songs and customs of various nations in Africa. See Fisher, *Negro Slave Songs in the United States,* pp. 66–79.

4. Frederick Douglass, *My Bondage and My Freedom* (New York, 1855), pp. 96, 97.

5. See Eileen Southern, *The Music of Black Americans* (New York: Norton and Co., 1971), pp. 30–45.

6. Quoted in Southern, *The Music of Black Americans,* p. 59.

7. See in Southern, *The Music of Black Americans,* pp. 27–29.

8. Early American Imprints, nos. 38, 39, series no. 2 (1801–1820).

9. *Soulfull Worship* (Washington, DC: National Office for Black Catholics, 1974); *The Spirit in Worship* (Cincinnati: Stimuli, 1978).

10. Confer "The Church at Prayer, A Holy Temple of the Lord," 4 Dec. 1983, the National Conference of Catholic Bishops, p. 23, no. 45; and Second Vatican Council, *Constitution on the Sacred Liturgy* (*Sacrosanctum Concilium*), 4 Dec. 1983, nos. 37–40.

11. "Somebody's Calling My Name," *Black Sacred Music and Social Changes* (Valley Forge, PA: Judson Press, 1979), p. 38.

12. The Bishops' Committee on Liturgy, "Music in Catholic Worship," rev. ed., 1983, pp. 3, 41.

13. *Understanding the New Black Poetry: Black Speech and Black Music as Poetic References* (New York: William Morrow, 1973), p. 44.

14. Rivers, *Soulfull Worship,* p. 39. See also *The Spirit in Worship,* pp. 14, 15.

15. "The Church at Prayer, A Holy Temple of the Lord," pp. 14, 15.

16. *The Spirit in Worship,* p. 22.

Part D
Church and Family

9

Black Church Community

In the traditional black community, the church is more than a body of believers in the Lord—it is an extended family.

Sister Thea was baptized Episcopalian and reared Methodist. Sometimes she went to the Episcopalian church with her father, other times to the Methodist church with her mother. Or she might worship at the Baptist church where, she recalled, she first burst into song at age three. At a very young age, Thea began searching for God in places where she thought God might be. In the autobiography Thea wrote as a novice, she said:

> Before I met Catholicism in 1947, I had tried the Methodist, Baptist, Episcopalian, Adventist, A.M.E. and A.N.E. Zion churches, but once I went to the Catholic church, my wanderings ceased. I knew I had found that for which I had been seeking. As Momma always says, "God takes care of babies and fools." I was baptized Roman Catholic by Fr. Justin Furman, ST, 8 June 1947, and the following day I made my first communion.

Thea gained a broad appreciation for black spirituality and for the variety of religious expression during her visits to all of those congregations. She became convinced that while Catholicism was right for her, other communities could teach her about creating community with her black brothers and sisters.

Mindful of the black bishops' 1984 pastoral letter on evangelization, in which they urged black Catholics to share their rich culture and

spirituality with the whole church and to become evangelizers themselves, Sister Thea described a model of black church community.

ᕙ\ᕗ ᕙ\ᕗ ᕙ\ᕗ

In the traditional black community, the church is more than a body of
believers in the Lord—it is an extended family. Many members may be
related by blood, but all elders are "mothers" and "fathers" in the
church. Godparents are especially respected in daily as well as church
life. Informal adoptions abound.

What black culture looks and sounds like is exemplified in more
and more churches where blacks are sharing their gifts. One such parish
is Holy Ghost in Opelousas, Louisiana, where visitors come from across
the country to see what it means to be black and Catholic.

With 10,000 members, Holy Ghost is the largest black parish in
the country. Parish leaders, including pastor Father Albert McKnight
and the 21-member parish council, work zealously to revitalize the people's faith.

As Father McKnight has said, "Black spirituality must embrace all
aspects of black life. We must learn to pray as if everything depended
upon God, and to work as if everything depended upon ourselves."

Sunday Mass, attended by some 3,000 people, is a family celebration enriched by the gifts of the people. Black music sets the tone. The
syncopated beat is accented by hand-clapping, foot-tapping, drums and
tambourines. The choir, readers, servers and celebrant move in rhythms
held sacred for generations as they praise the Lord with body and song.

Holy Ghost has seven choirs with members of all ages. Some of the
songs come from slave days: "Go Down, Moses," "Wade in the Water,"
"Swing Low, Sweet Chariot." The music also includes traditional hymns
and compositions by parishioners.

The service is alive, yet contemplative; participatory and sponta-
neous, yet in accordance with liturgical norms.

The celebrant enunciates the Gospel in the idiom of the people,
with drama, energy and intensity. His message relates to their daily
lives—poverty, racism, black pride and family values, support for the
hungry, the example of Martin Luther King.

"Let the Church Say 'Amen!'" originally appeared in *Extension* (Mar.–Apr. 1987):
10–11.

The people respond—an elder says "Hallelujah! Thank you, Jesus," and a teenager raises her hand in affirmation. At the Sign of Peace, priest and people move around the church, embracing.

The church art, created by sculptor Joe Shallow and painter Donald Alexander, both parishioners, reflects black life and experience. Jesus, Mary, Joseph, the disciples, and the figures in the Stations of the Cross resemble local people, with dark skin and curly hair. Red, black and green—Pan-African colors—adorn the altar and vestments to express black pride and solidarity with all African people.

After the two-hour celebration, the parishioners remain to visit and take care of church business. It is evident that they have been revived and renewed by worshipping together.

But to be black and Catholic extends beyond the liturgy. It includes supporting the extended family and being committed to the work of the Church. At Holy Ghost, workshops train parishioners to live out their Christian faith in ministry, liturgy, religious education, and leadership. For example, more than 50 Eucharistic ministers visit the sick each week. . . .

Holy Ghost Church is immersed in the life of the local black population. The parish operates a number of community programs such as a credit union and consumer co-op supermarket, housing for the elderly and handicapped, and counseling services. Despite the poverty of the area, the parish manages to be self-supporting.

. . . The Faith is lived by the people, enlivened by spirituality, and responsive to the needs of black people. As a result, black youths are finding new identity in the Church, parishioners are dedicating themselves to evangelization, people are returning to the Faith and asking others to join them.

Holy Ghost parishioners, echoing the words of Pope Paul VI to the peoples of Africa, say, "We are giving our gift of blackness to the whole Church. Let the Church say 'Amen.'"

10

Family

If we are not family, we can't become Church.

Sister Thea was convinced that "as we spend more time talking together, singing together, praying together, playing and working together, we grow to be family and community and Church" (p. 153).

Yet, she also insisted, "We have to plan ways and means to facilitate the kind of sharing that promotes that kind of growth" (p. 153).

In 1985, she edited *Families: Black and Catholic, Catholic and Black,* a book of readings, resources, and activities to help people become family, community, and church together. Thea's words and diagrams intimately connect black family and church.

From the Introduction

This book . . . assumes that the Black family is alive and well. It assumes further that we as a people need to find ways old and new to walk and talk together; to bond more surely; to extend family more widely and effectively, so that no one is fatherless, motherless, sisterless, or brotherless; so that no one lacks the life-sustaining human support of family.

The excerpts in this chapter are reprinted from *Families: Black and Catholic, Catholic and Black* (Washington, DC: United States Catholic Conference, 1985).

It attempts to help us maintain and strengthen Black rootedness, Black traditions and rituals whereby faith and values are transmitted and celebrated in family, in extended family, in intimate person-to-person exchange—mother to son, grandchild to grandpa, play brother to younger sister, friend to friend, member to member, and family to family. . . .

This book is also for people of any color or culture who have chosen to be family with us, to join with us and walk with us and minister with us. We hope that it will help them to get to know us better.

It is designed for people who come into our communities to be Church with us, but who do not understand, sometimes do not realize they do not understand, and sometimes do not seem to want to understand what we think, feel, believe, and love about family, community, and Church. . . .

Too often, white people come to us with answers to our problems. They don't bother to try to find out who we are, how we think, and what we're about. Too often, people who come to help do not realize that Black family is alive and well and that even when broken, even when hurting, it fosters deep faith and forges strong bonds. (P. 11)

Family, Community, Church

Everybody needs family. We start with a basic human need for family and for one another. We realize that one father, one mother are not enough: that families need the support of other families, and so we seek ways of bonding, nourishing, and healing.

We become community when families share values and needs. This bonding strengthens and nourishes us. The love that makes us community also makes us truly Church.

The Church formalizes and sacralizes bonding in matrimony, nourishing in Eucharist, the healing and anointing, the forgiving and reconciliation, so that our Sacraments are fulfilling of the kind of strength and support that families find in loving one another and in establishing community among themselves.

The popes have said that "the home is the domestic Church": that we are the Church. . . . Family feeds the Church and [the] Church necessarily feeds family. If we're not Church at home, we can't be Church when we go to church. If we are not family, we can't become Church. (P. 63)

Diagram of Shared Faith, Values, Love

Look at the word *family* at the bottom of the diagram on page 75. See how the life of community and Church radiate from family. If we nurture faith, values, and love in the family, then we can nurture faith, values, and love in the community and the Church.

Traditions and rituals that embody that faith, values, and love have to be worked on, and so we have family histories, memories, prayer, and catechesis, and celebrations as well as family dreams, goals, and plans. In faith we remember our history; we remember that we've come this far by faith. We celebrate that faith in our liturgies. We pass on our values when we dream and plan and work together. We celebrate the love we bear for one another in family fun, being together, enjoying one another, and in family ministry. We minister to our family, we minister within our family, we minister within the Black community. We, as Church, minister to our brothers and sisters, wherever we find them.

Family is the basic raw material from which community and Church can be formed. Family is the model of Church.

. . . Traditions and rituals of family, community, and Church embody faith, values, and love and provide life-giving connection with our past, vitality and comfort to our present, and hope and courage for our future. (P. 64)

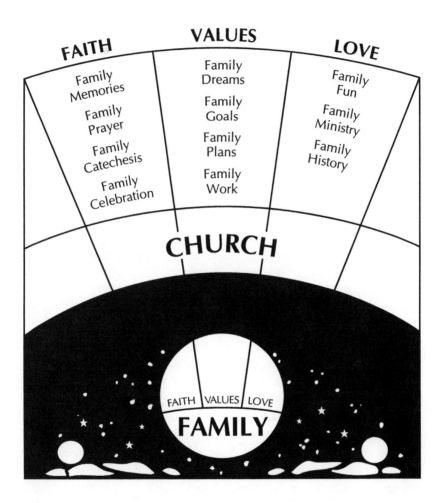

11

Women in the Church

Sharing life and faith and love is all our business, but in a special way and by a special calling—giving life, sustaining life, sharing life have always been life for women.

On several occasions, Sister Thea spoke about the special calling of women in the church: "giving life, sustaining life, and sharing life." The following speech was taken from her handwritten notes.

When I was a little girl in Canton, Mississippi, I went to those old black churches, and I learned what they called the old-time religion. I wanted to grow up so I could be a preacher.

Now you know women can't preach in the Catholic church. But that's not bothering me this morning. I can't preach in the church. Women can't preach in the Catholic church. But I can preach in the streets. I can preach in the neighborhood. I can preach in the home. I can preach and teach in the family. And it's the preaching that's done in the home that brings life and meaning to the Word your priest proclaims in his official ministry in the pulpit. . . .

It's Women's Day at Saint Clement Pope Church. We've come into the Lord's house in prayer and in community to honor the women. And when we honor the women, we honor you, too, men and children, because we honor your mothers and wives and lovers and sisters and daughters, aunts and nieces, and friends.

I invite all of you to pause a moment and bring to mind the women who gave you life, who nurtured you, who gave you light and laughter and faith and love. Did those women preach, did they teach, did they testify, did they witness?

Charles de Foucauld once said that every Christian is called to shout the Good News of the Lord Jesus Christ from the rooftops, not in words, but in life. We're all called to preach, to shout the Good News by our lives. Never too young, never too old to share life, faith, and love. A few years ago you hardly ever heard of people getting senile in the black community. [They were] too busy preaching, too busy teaching, too busy testifying and witnessing, too busy sharing life, faith, and love. An old song says, "Keep so busy serving my Master and God fur to die."

Sharing life and faith and love are all our business, but in a special way and by a special calling—giving life, sustaining life, sharing life have always been life for women. Married or single, young or old, rich or poor, in sickness and in health, in life and in death, so long as we have breath and being, we are called to be life-givers and life-nourishers and life-sustainers.

In the scriptural reading for today from the Book of Deuteronomy, we heard Moses tell the people to hear the statutes, observe the teachings, keep the commandments, and they will be wise and intelligent, and God will be close to them. Isn't that what your Mama told you? or your grandmother, aunt, or whoever mothered you in the Spirit? . . .

The Word of God became Incarnate. We are called to preach that word day by day by day—in our homes, in our families, in our neighborhood—to bear witness, to testify, to shout it from the rooftops with our lives.

Ladies, we are called to plant that Word in the minds and hearts and souls of our children, husbands, lovers, fathers, brothers, uncles, nephews, and friends. We don't have to worry about deception and hypocrisy. . . . They know when our witness is the fruit of our effort and struggle and sincerity.

God has called to us to speak the word that is Christ, that is truth, that is salvation. And if we speak that word in love and faith, with patience and prayer and perseverance, it will take root. It does have power to save us. Call one another! Testify! Teach! Act on the Word! Witness!

12

Black Catechesis

To bear good fruit, catechesis must be rooted in the spirituality of the people and couched in the language they best understand.

In her presentation "Spirituality: The Soul of the People," before the National Black Sisters' Conference in 1982, Sister Thea outlined specific directives to the catechists who would bring the Good News to her people.

Catechesis is both a formal and informal process of faith nurturance. . . .

Words, images, symbols, figures, stories, which express the spirituality of a people carry a freight of cognitive, affective, and volitional meanings developed and verified through long years of association and celebration. They are able to speak with eloquence to the minds, hearts and wills of a people. . . .

To bear good fruit, catechesis must be rooted in the spirituality of the people and couched in the language they best understand. It must also be in touch with their reality. Like Black Spirituality, catechesis must assume a common reality.

There is a common history—a brutal and violent one. There is a shared culture—and many different strands but common threads throughout. There is the recognition of a common parentage and a common relationship, and hence, a common spirit. (Cyprian

Davis, "The Black Contribution to a North American Spirituality," *New Catholic World* 225 [July–Aug. 1982]: 181)

Effective catechesis shares word and faith as it relates to this common experience and this common hope. Black catechesis, like Black religious songs, sermons, plays, and stories, relate that common identity, experience and hope to the Biblical Word in order to make that Word real and effective for Blacks today. Black Spirituality is biblical, Black catechesis is, therefore, necessarily biblical. It "lifts up the Word." It reads, proclaims, contemplates, sings, dramatizes, celebrates, wrestles with the Word. It looks at the Old Word until it becomes again startlingly new. Its elaborations are clearly designed to help the seeker see, hear, smell, feel and taste the reality of the biblical situation that is revealed today, right now. . . .

A catechesis that truly engages people speaks to the whole person. The Word that is ours to speak must be spoken the way that the people speak to themselves: Say it, sing it, pray it, play it, do it, be it. Combine comfort with the challenge, warmth with the definitiveness, wit with the seriousness, and a "good time" with the business at hand. Black catechesis demands energy of delivery. A catechesis that doesn't enliven catechists will certainly not energize those catechized.

Catechists, as messengers of the Good News of the Lord Jesus Christ, must find ways and means of knowing the spirituality of the people with whom they walk the journey of faith. They must understand and affirm the perceptions and responses of the people to God, self and others while challenging and being challenged by the people who have a Word that is their own to speak.

For people who are culturally Black, Black catechesis *is* effective catechesis. It is rooted in Black Spirituality. It is biblical. It is Christ-centered. It is contemplative. It leans upon the presence and the power of God. It is affective, feeling the pain of the world and seeing God as the cause of joy. It stresses the Christian responsibility to witness, to serve, to "make a way out of no way."

Black Spirituality is molded by the reality of the Black experience. Catechists who listen with prayerful reverence will learn to understand and appreciate that Spirituality. Catechists who understand can touch and empower the Black people, can be at home with them, can move Black people and be moved by them to incarnate the Inviolable Word that is "Christ among us." Such understanding is necessary to all who share the light of faith. (Pp. 92–94)

Part E
The Richness of Diversity

⟋⟍ 13 ⟋⟍

The Richness of Our Diversity

If I begin to believe that we are all alike, look at what I'm going to miss: the richness, beauty, wholeness, and harmony of what God created.

Thea learned to appreciate the richness of cultural diversity early in her life. When she taught at Viterbo College, Sister Thea conducted workshops for children about the culture of African Americans and Wisconsin Native Americans. People from both cultures came to assist her in these programs during the summer school sessions. Thea also formed a troupe of students from several cultures that performed multicultural music, drama, and dance in the La Crosse area.

Then in 1978, Thea returned home to Canton. She went south to care for her elderly parents, but she also wanted to be busy doing other things. She asked Bishop Joseph Brunini of the Jackson Diocese if he would hire her for a special apostolate dear to both their hearts—to be consultant (later director) for the Office of Intercultural Awareness.

Pamo Bauer of *Extension Magazine* described Thea's approach to ministry this way:

She teaches about Jesus to children and adults through song and poetry. She works to bring white, black, Hispanic and Indian peoples together through their common love of God. She uses literature, song, and dance to engage the different racial and ethnic groups in the diocese to appreciate each other. "Where we share faith together we really begin to embody Christ's vision," she said. ("Invitation to Sing" [Jan. 1984]: 6)

A yearly Extension Society grant made it possible for Thea to travel to elementary schools and high schools to present her one-woman show of scriptural singing and narrative to students and teachers. She and a special children's choir gave concerts throughout the diocese. Thea went wherever she was invited to teach that all of God's children are uniquely valuable and loved by God.

As the good news of Sister Thea's presentations spread, the scope of her audience expanded. Before long, she was speaking and singing throughout the United States, in the Caribbean, in Canada, and in Africa.

In two unpublished writings found among her papers, Sister Thea soundly rejected the idea that we are all alike and dismissed the relevance of the "melting pot."

ᏇᏇ ᏇᏇ ᏇᏇ

In the beginning, when Native America was here, we had Winnebago people, Navaho people, Cheyenne, Iroquois, you name it.

These people prided themselves in their difference—their diversity—in customs, dress, language, and governmental structure, but they came together as friends.

The history of our country is a history of diversity—Portuguese explorers, Spanish conquistadors, French traders, English settlers, African slaves, Italian immigrants, Irish immigrants, German scientists, Filipino students, Vietnamese refugees, Saudi Arabian merchants and investors—groups of people coming here, knowing who they were, remembering who they are.

Still, folks would try to convince you that we are all alike.

If you believe that, you don't need to bother about multicultural pluralism. We are not all alike. Emphatically NO! We do not look alike. We do not sing, dance, pray, play, think, cook, eat, wash, clean, chew, laugh, dress, or spit alike.

Asians are not like Europeans, are not like Africans. Irish are not like Italians, are not like French. Africans are not like Afro-Americans. Black folks are not alike. Folks from Louisiana are not like any other people in the world. Praise the Lord, we are not alike.

If I begin to believe that we are all alike, look at what I'm going to miss: the richness, beauty, wholeness, and harmony of what God created.

When I talk to little children, I always say:

You see this hand. It has five fingers. You know why God gave you five fingers? God gave you five fingers because there are five kinds of people. And you don't want to forget anybody. There are black people, brown people, white people, red people, and yellow people. And that's very convenient because if you keep your hand with you, and count on your fingers, you'll never forget anybody.

The melting pot meant trying to develop a common culture according to the Euro-Caucasian model: black, red, brown, yellow, and all the other people were supposed to "get with it" and assimilate. They found themselves acceptable insofar as they sacrificed their ethical and cultural uniqueness.

The minority people had to learn to walk like white folks, talk like white folks, work like white folks, play like white folks, spit and stand, pray and laugh like the majority, and that wasn't fun. They had to assimilate the values of the majority, and that wasn't healthy.

So the black and yellow and red and brown and Korean and Spanish and all the rest of the "ishes" were melted down and everybody came out half gray. We didn't like that. The minority people didn't like that.

So the people of the country—the black people, the red people, the brown people, the yellow people, and so many other minorities—began to think: To heck with the melting pot! If you want to melt and fit into my mold, if you want to adopt my values and way of life, go right ahead, but don't expect me to melt to fit yours.

As for melting and coming out gray, we refuse. If people choose the melting pot, that's fine. The whole idea of the melting pot is unhealthy for people like me.

We think it's unhealthy for you, too.

❧ 14 ❧

Reclaiming Black History

Knowing the wisdom of our ancestors who did with us what Mary and Joseph had done, we present our history and our lives before the altar and say thank you to God.

Sister Thea was committed to multicultural education, but she understood particularly well that African Americans needed to reappropriate black history and culture. Sister Thea helped found the Institute of Black Catholic Studies at Xavier University in New Orleans, and she served on the faculty. She specialized in training those ministering among black people, and she taught a popular course on the spirituality of black literature with Joseph A. Brown, SJ.

In an article in the *New Orleans Times Picayune,* Mary Queen Donnelly reported Thea's views about the Institute's mission:

> For years the white Catholic Church imposed its Caucasian methodology on black Catholics. You see, we don't want to change the sacraments. We don't want to change the theology of the church. We just want to express that theology within the roots of our black spiritual culture. ("Nun Brings Black Roots into Church," 14 Aug. 1988)

Sister Thea's two trips to Africa added to her appreciation of her people. In 1985, she attended the Forty-third International Eucharistic Congress held in Nairobi, Kenya. This trip was a gift from some two hundred American friends, students, and colleagues. On this occasion, Thea also visited Zimbabwe and Nigeria. Deeply moved by this opportunity to reconnect with her ancestral homeland, Thea remarked:

One of the most moving things for me is the realization that my sisters, mothers and fathers in Africa recognize black Americans as belonging to Africa. These people received me warmly and went out of their way to help me experience their culture in its various forms.

I am grateful to them for making me realize in a new way that I am an African American. . . . I feel a responsibility to share in every way I can the insight, beauty, wholeness and spirituality I saw in the African people with my American brothers and sisters of all colors. (Beatrice Njemanze, "Sister Bowman Touches Her African Roots," *Mississippi Today* [13 Sept. 1985]: 7)

In 1988, Sr. Norma Angel invited Thea to conduct a one-week workshop on racism for the Maryknoll sisters in Kenya and Tanzania. In her Christmas letter for that year, Thea wrote:

I found myself renewed by the scenic beauty, art, music, dance, drama, and prayer of the people. They truly ministered to me. We shared story and laughter and tears. With my bald head [from chemotherapy], I was mistaken for Maasai, even by the Maasai. It was a good feeling. . . . [It] made me feel overwhelmingly welcomed and at home.

Thea's pride in her heritage also stood out in her interview with CBS correspondent Mike Wallace for "60 Minutes." The filming took place on Hill Street in Canton where Thea grew up. Gazing down her street, she commented, "When I work with my kids, I say, 'black is beautiful,' and I make them say to themselves, 'I am beautiful.' Until they have found the beauty in themselves, they cannot appreciate the beauty in others." In a letter written to a friend, Thea rejoiced that sixty million people in five continents had heard her say, "We believe in God, in ourselves, in the future, and in the possibility of working together to make this troubled world a better and more joyful place for all of us."

Asked to speak to the people of Saint Columba Church on the Feast of the Presentation of Jesus in the Temple, Sister Thea used the occasion to celebrate black history.

ᎾᏇ ᎾᏇ ᎾᏇ

On this Feast of the Presentation of Jesus in the Temple, it is fitting that we call to mind black history and black life. The lesson to be learned today is that the hopes of our hearts and the labor of our lives are as precious to us as the life of Jesus was to his people.

Some two thousand years ago, Mary and Joseph did what the wisdom of their cultural and faith traditions told them to do. Today we acknowledge the wealth and the worth of our lives as the wisdom of cultural and faith traditions tells us to do.

Mary and Joseph presented Jesus in the Temple to give thanks for a male child. You see, they lived at a time in human history when a male child meant that the life of the family would live on through the eldest son. Their history taught them that a male child made the family more secure: He could work; he could build; he could manage the farm; he could tend the livestock; he could protect them from their enemies. Through this child, all that they held sacred was immortalized in the next generation.

Mary and Joseph's cultural and faith traditions told them to go to the Temple and give thanks to God for their child—a child whose life was an extension and an expression of their own lives. Their cultural traditions told them that they would live on through the child. Their faith traditions told them that the child was a gift from God. Listening to the wisdom of their history, Mary and Joseph presented Jesus in the Temple.

It is fitting that we call to mind black history and present the legacy of black life to God on this Feast of the Presentation. Like Mary and Joseph, we are doing today what the wisdom of our cultural and faith traditions have told us to do, for we live at a time in human history when it is clear that we need to remember the heritage that lives on is us.

Black history has given the world black men and black women who could work. They worked for freedom while they were treated like slaves. In their memory, we present our humble beginnings in America, and we give thanks to God.

Our history has given us black men and black women who could build. They built a sense of black dignity, even when society denied their worth. In their memory, we present our humanness, and we give thanks to God.

Our history has given us black men and black women who could manage the hardships of life. They managed to guide and prepare their children to make a contribution for the betterment of all human life. In their memory, we present the labor of our love, and we give thanks to God.

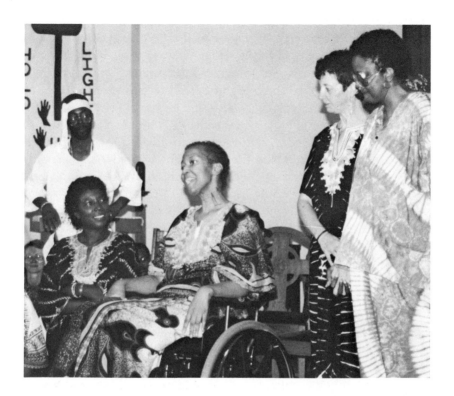

Our history has given us black men and black women who could tend to the wounds inflicted by evil: They could mend a broken heart; they could hang onto a battered woman; they could overcome rejection; they could look beyond prejudice; they could find new strength in the face of adversity. In their memory, we present the legacy of black life, and we give thanks to God.

We are an extension and an expression of their lives. It is fitting that we present our history before the altar and give thanks to God. Our cultural traditions have taught us that the wisdom of those who went before us lives on in our lives. Our faith traditions have taught us that what was noble in our ancestors and what is sacred in our black humanness are gifts from God. Just like Mary and Joseph, we have gathered today to present what is most precious to us to God.

It didn't matter to Mary and Joseph that their child was born in a stable. They took Jesus to the Temple anyway. It didn't matter to Mary and Joseph that their child was ridiculed by those who didn't appreciate his heritage. They took Jesus to the Temple anyway. It didn't matter to Mary and Joseph that their child would have to journey to Jerusalem without the comfort of a fine carriage or the distinction of a royal robe. They took Jesus to the Temple anyway. It didn't matter to Mary and Joseph that when they got to the Temple it was only a simple old man and a feeble old woman who recognized the presence of God in their child. They didn't need the recognition of the high priest or the approval of the chief magistrate to know that Jesus was a gift from God.

It seems to me that our ancestors had a "Mary and Joseph way of looking at things." It didn't matter to our ancestors that their children were born in the stable of a hostile society. They shared their belief in a God who could make a way out of no way. It didn't matter to our ancestors that their children would be ridiculed by those who couldn't appreciate their heritage. They taught us to walk tall anyway.

It didn't matter to our ancestors that their children would have to journey toward a life worth living on a perilous road. They focused our eyes on the victory anyway. They encouraged our dreams anyway. They sparked our imagination anyway. They forgave us our wrongs anyway. They celebrated our successes anyway.

And it didn't matter to our ancestors that most often they were the only ones who recognized the presence of God in black life. They didn't need the approval of somebody else to know that we, too, are made in the image and likeness of God.

Just like our ancestors, we got to hold on to a "Mary and Joseph kind of faith." We've got to hold on to a "Mary and Joseph way of looking at things." We've got to stop being ashamed that our history included slavery. We didn't enslave ourselves. Somebody else enslaved us. Let the people who created slavery answer to God for it, and let us thank God for the cultural and faith traditions that enabled us to overcome it.

You can be sure that Mary and Joseph were not ashamed of the stable in Bethlehem. They didn't choose it. They didn't ask for it. They knew they didn't deserve it. They let somebody else answer to God for the stable while they thanked God for their child.

We've got to stop assuming all the blame and guilt for the failures of our people. We didn't shape human history by ourselves. For every opportunity we missed, another one was denied. And for every opportunity that was handed to us, we created another one ourselves. Oh, yes, we have plenty of reasons to plead for forgiveness, but we also have plenty of reasons to praise God with thanks.

We've got to stop forgetting the contributions that nonblacks have made to black life. There is truth and goodness in the heritage of every cultural group. As we gather to celebrate the best in ourselves, we welcome and acknowledge the best in all humanity. Our celebration does not profess that we are better than other people. Our celebration is our way of joining hands with every person who seeks the Lord with an open heart.

At the same time, let us not be so awed by the gifts of others that we forget to marvel at the gift of ourselves. We present our history and our lives before the altar with gratitude and thanks. For it was through us that God gave the world Martin Luther and Coretta Scott King, whose vision and sacrifice have shown the power of good over evil. Through us, God gave the world Eubie Blake and B. B. King, whose jazz and blues mark the time to the seasons of all human life. Through us, God gave the world Langston Hughes and Alice Walker, whose poetry and praise have given a voice to what is noble in every human heart. Through us, God gave the world Booker T. Washington and Mary McLeod Bethune, who taught us that we can make a better tomorrow for everybody by making the most of ourselves today.

God has spoken to the world through us. He has made himself present to the world through us. So we gather in God's house, just as Mary and Joseph did, to give praise with our thanksgiving. Knowing the wisdom of our ancestors who did with us what Mary and Joseph had done, we present our history and our lives before the altar and say thank you to God.

15

Preparing Children for a Multicultural World

If our children are to be adequately prepared for life in a pluralistic, multiethnic, multicultural world, they must learn to understand and appreciate the basic religious traditions of the persons with whom they live and work.

Sister Thea saw religious and cultural variety as a gift and a challenge to Catholic schools. In an article written for the National Catholic Educational Association (NCEA), Thea outlined her ideas about preparing children to live in a multicultural world.

I recall with gratitude the experiences of my youth. At the age of twelve I escaped from a segregated public school system plagued with poverty, overcrowding, under-staffing and discouragement to find academic challenge, support and motivation, tailored instruction and an undreamed richness of educational resource, both human and material, at Holy Child Jesus Catholic School in Canton, Mississippi.

"Religious and Cultural Variety: Gift to Catholic Schools" is reprinted from *The Non-Catholic in the Catholic School* (Washington, DC: NCEA, 1984 and 1987), pp. 20–25.

The vast majority of the students were Baptist, Methodist, Holiness. There were at most two dozen Catholics in a student population of 180. Holy Child was a good place to be. We loved our teachers (all white nuns, Franciscan Sisters of Perpetual Adoration from Wisconsin) because they had first loved us. They worked with our parents. They worked with our families and friends. They worked with the Churches to "help us help ourselves."

For a handful of Catholics, for devout Protestants, for the children of a surprising number of ministers, deacons, elders and evangelizers, and for children who rarely went to any church, the Catholic school was a graced and grace-filled environment.

We all went to Mass each week, sang in the choir, learned, if we wished, to serve Mass (boys only) or to care for vestments and altar (girls only). We all prayed before every class. We all studied catechism. With Father Gilbert and Father Justin, religion class was a time to be anticipated and treasured—stories of Jesus and the saints, songs and prayers, and Catholic doctrine. Our pastors loved us. They entertained us as they taught us.

Some of my friends and schoolmates developed insights and skills (reading, thought, judgment, song) which enabled them to become young leaders in the Protestant churches of Canton.

I was drawn to examine and accept the Catholic faith because of the day-to-day lived witness of Catholic Christians who first loved me, then shared with me their story, their values, their beliefs; who first loved me, then invited me to share with them in community, prayer and mission. As a child I did not recognize evangelization at work in my life. I did recognize love, service, community, prayer and faith.

And now thirty-five years later, among the early students of Holy Child Jesus School I am in touch with Catholic parents and teachers, with Baptist and Methodist, Holiness and Adventist parents, teachers, preachers, exhorters, deacons, trustees and ministers of music. Thirty-five years later, embracing, as we do, a variety of religious traditions, we agree that our years in the Catholic school strengthened our faith and enriched our lives.

At the age of sixteen, I left Holy Child Jesus for high school in Wisconsin. There I was the only "convert," the only Southerner, the only Black in a totally white, Northern, Catholic school environment. I met high school students, young adults, even teachers who have never worked, played, prayed or even talked with persons of other faiths. Nobody seemed to know or care about "my Black/Southern/down-home/

Gospel-oriented faith" or inculturation. I was loved and accepted. Still, secretly, I felt very much the outsider. That was thirty years ago, but we know that in some areas Catholic schools with homogeneous populations still exist.

Fortunately for all, however, an increasing number of children from a wide variety of religious, cultural, racial, national and socio-economic backgrounds are now enjoying the advantages of Catholic education. Students, parents, faculty and staff from a variety of cultural and religious traditions are often able not only to accept but also to support and further the philosophy, purpose and goals of Catholic education. Their presence can only serve to enrich the community that is the Catholic school.

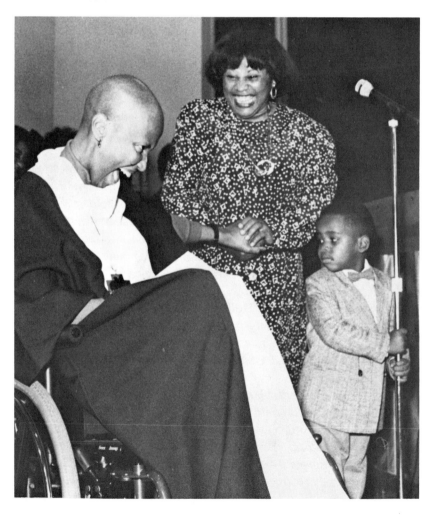

If our children are to be adequately prepared for life in a pluralistic, multiethnic, multicultural world, they must learn to understand and appreciate the basic religious traditions of the persons with whom they live and work. When we as Catholic students, parents, faculty, staff, administrators, approach believers of other religious traditions with appreciation and reverence we realize their faith and faithfulness. We are inspired by their convictions. We are broadened by their perspectives and challenged by their questions. We learn from their religious experience. As we work with them for peace and justice, as we cooperate with them in feeding the hungry, clothing the naked, teaching the ignorant, empowering the oppressed, we truly share the Good News of the Kingdom.

The presence of persons (students, parents, teachers) from the variety of religious and cultural traditions within the close community of the Catholic school can provide for all our children from their earliest years a supportive environment in which to grow in mutual understanding as well as the opportunity for true ecumenical dialogue and collaboration on an on-going basis. . . .

If we reflect together on the specific traditions which we embrace, our own ideas, values, and convictions are clarified, redefined and confirmed; our differences are understood; our commonalities are celebrated, and we are empowered for life in an ecumenical age and a pluralistic society.

. . . Consider, for example, what we as a Catholic educational community might learn from:
• Black American holistic and celebratory spirituality;
• Asian techniques of meditation and prayer;
• the Hispanic tradition of home and family-centered religious education and celebration;
• traditional Native American reverence for all creations of the Great Spirit . . .
• the Buddhist and Mennonite practice of dedicating one or more years of young adulthood to full-time service in monastery or missions;
• the Muslim insistence upon the relationship of religious faith and active commitment to sociopolitical involvement. . . .

The presence of students from the variety of cultural and religious tradition challenges us as Catholics:
• to free ourselves from the assumptions that the Good News is limited to any institutional denominationalism;
• to develop a catechesis that is truly multicultural;

- to develop a liturgy so meaningful, so authentically celebratory, so wedded to reality of life that it can communicate to any person of faith;
- to revitalize our religious education and to speak the Word in language that is meaningful and life-giving to all members of the Catholic school community;
- to provide liturgical and paraliturgical ecumenical experiences utilizing the giftedness of *all* our students;
- to share and celebrate the religious insights and expressions of *all* members of the school community;
- to free our Catholic Christian teachings from the cultural accretions of any single place or time;
- to insure that ritual, gesture, music, preaching are wedded to the real life and culture of all the students;
- to abandon the Catholic ghetto mentality which sometimes seems to operate on the assumption that our faith cannot withstand the challenge of dialogue or even conversation.

. . . If we are convinced that all our students "bring with them a rich heritage and contribute significantly to the environment within the school," then we are bound to give flesh and substance to our conviction.

If all members of the school community are to recognize and respond to one another's needs and the needs of the community, school-sponsored programs of service must be participatory rather than paternalistic; must see the needy as brothers and sisters, not strangers or objects of beneficence; must be designed to empower the needy to help themselves and to contribute by their struggles and experience to the common good. . . .

❧ 16 ❧

Martin Luther King, Jr.

We have gathered here to remember and to celebrate Dr. Martin Luther King, Jr. But to remember without resolve is empty, and to celebrate without intent is mockery.

Thea was the granddaughter of slaves, and even though her father, a doctor, made an above-average income for a black man of his time, she knew racial discrimination firsthand. Growing up in the South, she could not avoid its ugly consequences.

Thea saw the effects of poverty and prejudice through her father's medical practice. Office hours frequently began at dawn, and she said:

> People had to come to see the doctor either before they went to work—and they would start work at 5, 5:30—or after work, 8 or 9 at night. . . . And my daddy would sometimes be paid in greens, or someone would work on his car. Once he got half a lamb. (Arthur Jones, "She sings a Ululu Song That Began in Africa," *National Catholic Reporter* [9 Sept. 1988]: 4)

In the autobiography that she wrote as a novice, Thea described the poverty surrounding her childhood:

> As a family, we knew nothing of society or bright lights. We always had the necessities of life and even occasional superfluities. My parents loved me and they have been as loyal as the dial to the sun. [But] during the first fifteen years of my life, I saw more of poverty, filth, disease, and suffering than many people see in a lifetime, and I learned that it is not a sacrifice to go without a few meals or bear a stench, fatigue, or a little dirt for someone you love. . . . I

think I can, with the help of divine grace, . . . promote the welfare of my neighbor if only I can learn to live with enthusiasm, to rejoice in God my Savior, to wake up in the morning and smile at God.

Thea experienced oppression in her town and neighborhood. For instance, Mississippi law during Thea's lifetime determined what land black people could own. As a result, Canton's black community was relegated to land so marshy, so filled with mosquitoes, land crabs, and frogs that it was named "Frog Hollow." A town ordinance even forced the black Catholic church—the Holy Child Jesus Mission—to build its entrance facing away from the street.

So when Thea spoke about the leadership of Rev. Martin Luther King, Jr., when she spoke about freedom and civil rights, she could speak with the passion that springs from personal experience.

On 17 January 1988, the Milwaukee Commission on Community Relations presented its fifth annual celebration of the life of Martin Luther King, Jr. Sister Thea not only delivered the main speech but also directed the choir.

Before the celebration, Thea led the choir rehearsal. Reporter Lyn L. Hartmann described Thea's instructions to the choir for the *Milwaukee Journal.*

You all are singing, and it's sounding real sweet. Use those voices like percussion instruments. African folks had the drums to fire the people with the spirit. You got all those big old chests, great big old lungs, great big old muscles, but I can't hear you. You're holding back on me.

There are two things I'm asking from you. I'm asking for your fine musicianship. But I'm also asking you for something that comes before that. Folks call it a primitive strength and energy. It has to come from the bottom of your feet, from the pit of your stomach, from your heart as well as your head.

It has to come from all the times when somebody beat you down. Is there anybody here who doesn't know that kind of experience?

Lock those arms and move with me. When we were down south during the marches, the people would lock those arms, so that when the dogs came, when the billy clubs came, so that when the rifle butts came, when the tear gas came, nobody would get lost and nobody would get hurt. Remember those days? . . .

Did you ever go to an old-time, back-in-the-woods, under-the-trees type of church? The elders would draw the spirit into the church. There was something about the old folks. They would start all kinds of synapses snapping. It's a kind of strength and power, that singing, that witnessing. It grips people at a level of heart and feeling and emotion. It's complete improvisation. People who know how to do it, know. . . . That's what I want from you. . . .

One of the things I want our singing to be able to say is that Martin Luther King wanted to be a scholar; he wanted to be a preacher. He didn't want to be out on the streets. When his people called him, he was a young man. He was 29 years old. But he saw people in need and he saw in himself an ability to try to effect change.

People keep saying, "Where's the next Martin Luther King?" We're all called, I think. We're called by our citizenship, by our membership in the human race. We're all called to free ourselves and to free one another. I want our singing to be able to convey that, not just to ourselves, but to our children and to our elders. . . .

When we walk together and work together and talk together and plan together, we make that dream come true. I might not be able to make it come true for the whole world, but if in my own sphere of influence I can work for better understanding, for more love and more harmony and happiness, then it does change the world. If I can find the hope and the faith in myself, then I can give hope and faith to the people who come into my world. . . .

Some of us walk around, and we think we're free. Some people think, well, I have a good job and my children are in school and the Klan is not at my door. Folks are not insulting me on a regular basis. But there's still the poverty, there's still the ignorance, there's still the aggression. It's not over. . . .

I want to remind all of us that to celebrate Martin Luther King without being real about the dream is sacrilege. If we don't intend to do something, it's a waste of time. I want our voices to say that I did try to feed the hungry, I did try to clothe those who were naked, I did try to visit those who were in prison. That's the message. That's the dream we celebrate.

You can't just give lip service to the message of Dr. Martin Luther King and what he did. You have to live the dream.

By living the dream, I bring joy to my life. And by living the dream, I share that joy. It's contagious. I really believe that. ("The Message of Music," 17 Jan. 1988)

Thea's talk at the "Martin Luther King: Seize the Vision" celebration proved to be the last time that she could stand to give a presentation. The day after it, she became very ill. The cancer had so invaded her lower back that henceforth she would make appearances only in a wheelchair, accompanied by her companion, Sr. Dorothy Ann Kundinger. But on that January day in Milwaukee, she delivered this tribute to Dr. King and this challenge to her listeners.

ᘓ\ᗯ ᘓ\ᗯ ᘓ\ᗯ

We have gathered here to remember and to celebrate Dr. Martin Luther King, Jr. But to remember without resolve is empty, and to celebrate without intent is mockery. Martin was a man, not perfect, flawed as we are flawed, determined, dedicated. Martin was an ambassador for justice, . . . an activist, an agitator. Call him what you will, he was willing to speak out, to march, to be jailed, to be cursed, to be spat upon, to be beaten and abused. He was willing to lay down his life for what he believed in. The grandson of a slave, he was able to talk with statesmen and politicians, the rich and the poor, the erudite and the illiterate, old people and little children, garbagemen and farmers, presidents and princes. [He was] preoccupied with that struggle for freedom, strengthened by his belief that God would lead the oppressed to freedom.

But we are not here to celebrate a man; we are here to celebrate a dream—a dream of freedom, a dream deeply rooted in the American dream. A dream so vital that it has drawn people of all lands to these shores. A dream that dares to say, "Give me your tired, your poor, your huddled masses yearning to be free." A dream that all men and women and children can find life and liberty and happiness and wholeness. Men, women, children—black, red, white, brown, yellow and all the colors and hues between—have lived, have died to make that dream a reality, have died to guarantee freedom for their children and their children's children for generations. We are here to celebrate not a man but a dream—a dream of freedom. My country, my country 'tis of thee I sing.

[Choir and assembly sang "America."]

Martin Luther King, in spite of everything, believed in that dream. The dream founded on faith in the humanity of humankind, in the ultimate triumph of justice and righteousness.

He was born in the South as some of you were. Born 15 January 1929, born middle class to educated people, having all the advantages of learning available to a black man, a black child at that time. But Martin was still the child of poverty and oppression and discrimination.

In 1954, when the Supreme Court ordered the desegregation of schools in this land, he was just twenty-five years old, pastor of Dexter Avenue Baptist Church.

In December 1955, when Mrs. Rosa Parks refused to give up her seat to a white passenger, he was twenty-six. At twenty-six, this man was called to lead his people, to lead a bus boycott for freedom, and for two years fifty thousand people did not ride a bus. Some of those folks will tell you that they didn't ride a car, they didn't ride a train, they didn't ride a plane, they didn't ride a bicycle because they were committed to freedom, and they wanted to teach their children the lesson of freedom.

In 1956, King's home was bombed, but that did not stop him.

In the 60s with prayer marches, sit-ins, freedom rides, nonviolent protests, and arrests in North Carolina, in Georgia, in Illinois, in Alabama, in Mississippi, and in California, Martin worked for freedom.

In 1963, at the age of thirty-four, Martin led the historic march on Washington for jobs and freedom. At the age of thirty-four, many of us would say he was a very young man. The march on Washington for jobs and freedom, for civil rights legislation, for integration in the public schools, for federal programs for training and placing unemployed workers, for fair employment practices. Does it sound familiar? Martin worked for voter registration, for desegregation on jobs, for decent educational opportunity for all the children.

In 1963, he worked with the Kennedys, and JFK was assassinated.

In 1964, together we won the civil rights law. Johnson began the war on poverty.

In 1965, Selma—you know, that march to Montgomery, black and white together, men and women and children of all races and all religions and all national persuasions. You know it—the bombs, the tear gas, the horses, the dogs, the faith and love and nonviolence.

All over this country, King helped to dramatize the plight of the poor, the plight of the disenfranchised, the oppressed and dispossessed. King called for help, a matter of conscience, he said, and attempts to arouse the deepest conscience of the nation.

In Milwaukee—some of you were here. In Milwaukee, that city to which so many black folks had fled for jobs, for better educational opportunity for their children, for better housing, you remember, don't you? So many of our people coming here to a land of opportunity. There was that long hot summer that drew the attention of the nation and the world to this place when men and women stood up and spoke out for justice, when adults demonstrated and were arrested and jailed, when the children hit the streets—the teenagers and the children—to struggle for justice. Three hundred people arrested—maybe some of you—four deaths! I mean it was a time when the people of Milwaukee knew how to take care of business. The National Guard was called in, and a curfew closed this city. And the world knew, and you know how the racist forces were, are, and ever will be afraid of that adverse publicity.

King continued to work against violence. He continued to work in the antipoverty campaign for jobs, for decent salaries, for decent working conditions, for fair employment practices, for education.

In 1968, planning that antipoverty march to Washington—Mexican Americans and Puerto Ricans, Native Americans and poor whites—to force the Congress to provide jobs and income for the poor. There was violence in our cities and violence on our campuses, and King attempted to unite the poor, to unite the unemployed and the disenfranchised, to bring together men and women of goodwill who believed in the American dream.

On 4 April 1968, when King was a very young man, when he was thirty-nine years old, he came to Memphis, Tennessee, to help encourage the garbagemen. I know you call them sanitation workers, but these were garbagemen. They handled the garbage and refuse of society. Martin King came into Memphis because it was thought that his presence would be a deterrent to violence. As he had lived in faith and for love, Martin Luther King died, and so today we celebrate the man and the dream.

But there is still violence; there is still unemployment; there is still inequality in hiring, in pay, and in housing; there is still hunger and greed and selfishness and oppression and fear. I read your papers. Nearly 40 percent of Milwaukee black residents live in poverty or near poverty. Black unemployment is the highest in the nation and in the four-county metropolitan area. Twenty years after your housing marches, the Milwaukee County suburbs remain remarkably white. The poor are still trying to deal with a rising teenage pregnancy rate, single parentage where children are not supported by the total family, total community. You know how it was in the old days. If a child had a baby, that child's family and the community would intervene, because a child can't raise a child, and how can you . . . ? Don't get me started now. . . .

You can talk about crime in these cities—you can talk about native rights in a city, in a state that prides itself on its Indian heritage. You can talk about the plight of the newest of our refugees. We, if we honor King, if we are to celebrate King, if we are to live the dream, we have to work together, all of us, work together for freedom for all of us, for all of God's children. To the affluent among us: Take back to your community the message that if a poor child is disadvantaged, everybody pays. You pay in welfare; you pay in crime; you pay in fear and anxiety. To the poor: Take back to your communities the message that you are able so long as you have your health and strength to demand of this city the opportunity that is yours, the opportunity to learn, the opportunity to earn. And you know what they used to say in the old days—if you know so much and you are so smart—each one teach one.

I read in one of your papers that Milwaukee is one of the most segregated metropolitan areas in the country. You have come together today to be about peace, to be about justice, to be about freedom, and to be about unity. And the celebration that we share is a mockery if the beauty we have shared we do not take back into our homes and our neighborhoods.

Twenty years ago in April, Martin Luther King died. If he had lived, he would be just fifty-eight years old. I ask you: Are you as dedicated to justice and freedom and peace as you were twenty years ago? Are you as willing to put your life on the line? Martin Luther King, Jr.—you heard it today—he seemed to know he would die for freedom and justice. He seemed to know he would die for the dream, and he told us what to say at his funeral. He said tell them that Martin Luther King, Jr., gave his life serving others, that Martin Luther King, Jr., tried to love somebody, that Martin Luther King, Jr., tried to feed the hungry, that he tried to clothe the naked, that he tried to visit those in prison, that he tried to love and serve humanity. That's the dream.

If I can help somebody as I pass along, then my living will not be in vain. Let us meditate on those words and carry them in our hearts and carry them into our homes, into our neighborhoods, and teach them to our children. That's the message, that's the dream.

[Choir and assembly sang "If I Can Help Somebody."]

If I can give, if I can love, if I can serve, if I can help. King said, "Love must not be based on what will happen to me if I am called upon to show love in action, but what will happen to the person in need if I do not help." Did you hear that? . . . What are you going to do, you see? What are you going to do? What will you do to help bring the people of this beautiful metropolitan area together so that they can talk with one another, walk with one another, play with one another, work with one another, and pray with one another, and begin to understand one another? What are you going to do? What are you going to do to teach somebody?

I'm from Mississippi. People wanted to come to Milwaukee to learn how to read. Well, look at your own illiteracy rates these days. What are you going to do to teach somebody? Can you help somebody find a job? What are you going to do for freedom and justice—you? Just because you are ten years old, don't think I'm not talking to you, and you are never too old to love. You are never too old to love somebody. We have come this far by faith and hope and love and determination and courage. We've come too far to turn around. We have come too far to sit down and become apathetic. We have come too far to be indifferent. We've come too far to let this city fall apart. But we have to celebrate our journey: we have to celebrate the dream and remind ourselves and remind our neighbors and remind the little children. Think about the people who have brought you this far.

[Choir and assembly sang "We've Come This Far by Faith."]

Martin Luther King, Jr., was a man of faith. He believed in God. He believed in himself. He believed in the humanity of humankind. He wrote:

> I have the audacity to believe that people everywhere can have three meals a day for their bodies, education and culture for their minds, and dignity, equality, and freedom for their spirit. I believe that what self-centered people have torn down, other-centered people—other-centered people like you—can build up. I still believe that one day mankind will bow before the altar of God and be crowned triumphant over war and bloodshed, and nonviolent redemptive goodwill will be proclaimed the rule of the land. I still believe that we shall overcome.

[Choir and assembly sang "We Shall Overcome."]

༄\ྀ 17 ༄\ྀ

Cosmic Spirituality:
Formation in a New Age

God's glory is revealed because we love one another across the barriers and boundaries of race, culture and class.

At the 1987 National Congress of the Religious Formation Conference, Thea urged those present to remember that they must form religious to minister in a multicultural, religiously plural society.

You are formation personnel. Your conference theme is cosmic spirituality. We think you're talking about the spirituality of the cosmos, the spirituality of the universe. You are helping men and women prepare themselves for life and ministry in a multicultural church and world. You're trying to help folks get in touch with the spirituality that is of us all. The majority of people in the Catholic church are not white, European, Caucasian. The majority of the people in the Catholic church are people of color. The majority of the people in the world are people of color. And it's the cosmos, the universe, the world in all its diversity spirituality for which we are preparing ourselves and our congregations. Cosmic spirituality means we're going to have to learn new languages.

Sister Thea presented "Cosmic Spirituality: No Neutral Ground" at the 1987 National Congress of the Religious Formation Conference in New Orleans.

We're going to have to learn new rhythm. We're going to have to learn new ways of glorifying the Lord. How can you teach your folks back home if you can't share a culture and spirituality that's different and unfamiliar? You can't learn culture or spirituality by reading a book. If you could, we'd all be better informed. We learn cultures and customs and languages of faith, we learn cosmic spirituality by *sharing,* by sharing prayer and song and ritual and story, by involving ourselves and participating, by giving and receiving. . . .

We invite men and women from the cultures of the world to come into our congregations. Men and women with roots in Asia, Africa, Australia, Latin America, Native America, and the islands. We invite them. They come from New Orleans or Canton, Mississippi, from Haiti or the Iroquois Reservation, from Mexico or El Salvador or the Philippines, from China, India, Vietnam, Nigeria, or Harlem. So often in formation and in community, their spiritual gifts and spiritual journeys are dismissed or ignored. Talk with the people of color in your congregations, in your formation programs. Ask them to what extent they believe that you are serious about understanding them—their history, their experience, their culture, their heritage, their art, their music, their styles of prayer, their styles of meeting, their songs, their dances, their modalities of relationship. To what extent are you serious about sharing their spirituality, their styles of life and prayer and relationship? Ask them how they feel in your congregation. Have you asked them lately?

When Jesus is among us, to work among us miracles of transformation and miracles of love, there is no neutral ground. Neutral ground becomes loving ground; loving ground becomes holy ground; holy ground becomes Kingdom ground. We are the children of the cosmos, the children of the universe. In this world of rapid transit; supersonic, interplanetary, sonar communication; computerized nuclear technology; robotics; some folk go to Europe, Australia, and Africa like we used to go to New Orleans and Chicago. We're children of the universe, called and sent to transform the cosmos.

Jesus is able. We believe he is a Waymaker, and when we come together in Jesus' name, we come for transformation. Cosmic spirituality means we come together, bring our gifts, bringing our histories, bringing our experience, bringing our positives and negatives, our arts, our skills, our teaching-learning methodologies—all of them—all that we have and all that we hold. Bearing and wearing our best, we come to the wedding feast, and we do as Jesus said, we draw the water. We carry it to the chief steward, and we testify to the miracle.

We become the miracle when we love one another. "God so loved the world that he gave his only begotten son so that whosoever believeth in him would not perish but would have everlasting life." And Jesus says to us, "As the Father has loved me, love one another." Now how can you love somebody you don't know? And how will you know if you do not study, if you do not sit at the feet of the elders, if you do not learn from the little children, if you do not read the books and see the plays and hear the music? How can you prepare for a world that's cosmic? How can you share a spirituality that shares Gospel values within the cosmos?

Jesus says, "As the Father loves me, I love you." And "As I have loved you, love one another." He doesn't say love anyone that looks like you, thinks like you, prays like you, dresses like you, talks like you. "Love one another as I have loved you. Greater love than this nobody has than to lay down life." You try to work with us sometimes. You get tired of us. You get discouraged with us. I remember when you were talking about going where you had never been before. You remember those days? Uh huh. And some of those folk who went where they had never been before never found themselves at home where they had never been before. They decided to go back home. That was a good idea.

Jesus said, "They will know that you are mine, because you love one another." When we love one another, we become the miracle. We witness to the miracle. We are transformed by his love, and the world beholds his glory in our transformation. Are you with me, church? . . .

We're talking about cosmic spirituality. We're talking about the independence and the interdependence of all the world's people. And if we take the Cana story seriously, we will be rocketed and ricocheted out of our old complacencies. Off neutral ground and onto Kingdom ground.

Jesus said to his mama his hour had not come. You know how we are. We sit around and wait for the hour. But Mary by her belief, by her faith, by her persistence, could call upon her son. "The modest waters saw their God and blushed." Jesus revealed his glory.

When you come into my community, my town, my world, will you see God's glory revealed? When you go to my brothers and sisters in beautiful Hawaii, will you see his glory? When you experience, when you share the hungers of Ethiopia, the blood flow of Guatemala and Nicaragua, will you see his glory revealed?

I want to take you way back. "Gimme that old-time religion." I have to praise the Lord the way I know how to praise the Lord. And as I bless his holy name, are you prepared to learn from me in your formation program?

You say, "Lord, teach us to pray." You taught me to pray. Are you ready to learn from me? You teach the people who come to you in formation. Do you learn from them the habits of prayer that they bring from their homes, from their cultures? Or do you try to remake them according to your mold and fashion? Do we come together to share bread, to share prayer, to *share* styles and modalities of faith and worship? Or do we always have to do things your way?

If I always have to come into your house and be a stranger, I might as well go home to my mama, or my daddy, my community, where they know me and love me. I'm talking about seminarians. I'm talking abut young women in formation who enter congregations where they don't find home. If you know what I'm talking about, say *Amen.*

I'm talking about my friend Marcy who said she never really felt like she prayed unless she prayed in Spanish, because her grandmothers and her aunts and her mother and her father taught her how to pray in Spanish. . . .

If you believe that the spirit that lived in Jesus, that the spirit that lived in the disciples, that the spirit that moved in the early church is the same spirit you receive in your baptism and confirmation, say *Amen.* If you believe that you, like Jesus, are called by the spirit to share the spirit in the world, to call forth the giftedness of God's people, say *Amen.* If you believe that God is able to work in all the brothers and the sisters, in the ones you customarily write off because they don't read right, they don't write right, they drink too much, they smoke the wrong thing, they don't walk right, they don't talk right, their sexual preferences are not in agreement with the ones you claim.

If you believe that God is able to transform the water of my reality into purist wine, if you believe there's nothing God can't do, let me hear you say *Amen.* . . .

The reality of the pain of being a "minority" must be acknowledged. The system has to identify folk with which our people can relate. The system can also identify a person within their own ranks who is willing to serve as a listener. So often black folk come in and they attempt to say, "This is my story; this is my song; this is my experience; this is the experience of my people in religious formation." And you know what we're told, "Well, must you be so sensitive, yeah, must you be so sensitive? You have a chip on your shoulder." Are you with me, church?

The goal of the system, the black community, and the candidate are essentially the same: to recruit, maintain, sustain black candidates so that the church may grow from the service of such individuals. Now I'm talking to you about the black community, and I'm talking to you about black candidates, but there are those among you who can talk to you about the needs of the Native American or the Hispanic or the Asian.

In this cosmic system where we find ourselves, Jesus calls red, black, white, brown, yellow and all the hues and colors between, the children of all Africa and Asia, and Central America and the islands, and Europe and North America. Jesus calls. He calls the young and the middle-aged and the geriatric generation too. We come together in this cosmic society needing love and security and nurturance and stability. Single, married, divorced, folks from nonfunctional families. Communities used to deny the problems.

"Only virgins of good reputation and good family were admitted." Now Jesus calls virgins of good repute, also victims of sexual abuse, child abuse, chemical abuse, violence and war; some who have been and perhaps are sexually, heterosexually, homosexually active, presenting the whole threat of AIDS in our formation programs; some people who are sexually preoccupied, misunderstood, misunderstanding, and grieving. Jesus calls college graduates, competent, experienced, effective, multi-degreed, traveled professionals, politicians, educators, administrators, health-care professionals. It's a cosmic world. Jesus calls to the diverse, and how often they find themselves misunderstood.

All my life my mama told me to stand up straight, hold up my head, and speak out. And what happens to the person in formation who dares to? We have the children among us of alienation and anger and frustration, of guilt and shame, men and women with unexpressed hopes and loves and yearnings, with feelings of separation and denial. Children of the universe, we come together in Jesus' name, and the only answer that we can offer to one another is the love that is found in the word of God, the love that is shared and celebrated in Jesus' name. Love, enunciated in a thousand languages, a thousand symbols, a thousand rituals, a thousand ways so that the giftedness and the heritage of the multiplicity of God's people becomes available to all of us and to the church that we call our home. . . .

To what extent are you ready to eat, to pray, to play, to work with the people of the universe? And if you haven't got time to play with us, to put your feet under the table and rest yourself a while, it is unlikely that you can share faith, life, and love with us. Jesus had time to spend at the wedding feast. He and his disciples were there because it was important to be there. . . .

We have come together in Jesus' name and we pray, Oh Father, give us the spirit of transformation that the water of our lives may become purest wine and that your glory may be revealed to all the brothers and sisters, to the whole cosmos, to the limits of the universe. God's glory is revealed because we love one another across the barriers and boundaries of race, culture, and class. We love not just in words but in food and in prayer and in song and dance and in learning and working together.

Let the church say *Amen.*

Part F
Living

18

The Loving Core
of Christian Living

Maybe I'm not making big changes in the world, but if I have somehow helped or encouraged somebody along the journey then I've done what I'm called to do.

In an interview with Catherine Browning of *Creation* magazine, Thea summarized many of her core beliefs about living. In the following excerpts, Thea talks about creation, reconciliation, love, and listening to God.

Creation: As I reflect upon some of the contributions you have made during your earthly pilgrimage I am deeply moved by your trust in the goodness of humanity. What, for you, is at the heart of this trust?

Bowman: I basically believe we are God's creation, made in God's image and likeness. So much of the trouble of the world is caused by fear, hurt, and ignorance. If we trust in humanity, if we teach, help, and reconcile each other, then we can love one another into life.

The interview excerpts in this chapter are reprinted from "Trusting the Prophetic Call," *Creation* [Nov.–Dec. 1989]: 19–21.

Faith, putting these into action makes it possible. I have seen it! I have seen the power of trusting people with low self-esteem, people who have hurt themselves, their families, the society. We hurt each other and our environment when we don't take time to understand and to appreciate one another's gifts. When we reach out, in faith and trust, we love one another into life.

Creation: . . . What gives you the strength and the courage to continue working for the betterment of the planet?

Bowman: I draw strength from the wisdom I gained in the black community that reared me. I was told "Nobody wants to see you looking sour." In every life there's pain, struggle, and obstacle. We have to learn to live with the pain, to walk in faith, and to work out our salvation. It takes courage, but if we work together and stay together, we can do it.

I've never aspired to do big things in life. I've tried to teach . . . that real, effective love changes things. Maybe I'm not making big changes in the world, but if I have somehow helped or encouraged somebody along the journey then I've done what I'm called to do.

Creation: How might we each more fully awaken and respond to the individual and collective roles we are here to fulfill?

Bowman: We have to take time to listen to God in Scripture, in nature, in our own heart, in our feelings, passions, and dreams. We have to listen to each other. . . . We have to take the *time* to listen and observe. We have to take the time to pray and dialogue together, no matter how poor, hurting, or weak we are. Then we can begin to effect change *here and now!* . . .

Creation: What do you see as the role the human species is here to play with the rest of creation? Where do you see humans fitting in with the animals, the forests, the oceans, the birds?

Bowman: From the spiritual tradition of the black community I learned that we are *all* God's creatures. Creation is a gift God shares with us. We have a responsibility to learn from nature how to live, to observe nature because it houses the lessons of life. We can learn from the way the ant works with his peers, how the bear lives in winter, how the tree grows tall, how the sun rises in fidelity, the way day follows night.

I grew up with people who taught us how to respect and appreciate nature, to study nature's secrets, to reverence the very soil beneath our feet. My people in the South were farmers and they learned patience. You can't rush the seasons; you can't call forth the rain.

They also learned not to waste! And that's something we all need to pay more attention to today! It's important not to take more than we need. Take your share and leave the rest for the others. If we live cooperatively the earth produces sufficiently to feed and shelter us all.

I believe in saving the whales and working for other environmental causes. But I am bothered by the amount of media attention given to birds, seals and whales when children are starving on this planet, when old people who have worked hard all their lives live in dire poverty, when even in the USA millions of people lack adequate food, shelter and medical care. I'm not saying we shouldn't be concerned about the whales. I'm just saying let's get our priorities straight. We possess the technology to feed everybody, to provide remedies for basic illness, to lower the high infant mortality rate, to relieve world hunger. We have to call each other to awareness of the suffering persons in the world. We have to help each other to wake up. People who control resources and wealth so often don't even know the poor who are displaced.

The earth is our mother. We come from her and we return to her. She's our home. When we destroy her we destroy ourselves. We are here as stewards of the earth. We have a responsibility to care for the earth *and* to care for the people who are poor and in need, regardless of their color, race, nationality or sex.

Creation: What helps to facilitate a feeling of oneness with the earth, a pride in and commitment to the future of our planet?

Bowman: I don't see myself as one with the earth. How can I? Earth is God's gift that I am expected to share. Earth is our mother. Earth is our home. When we destroy the Earth we destroy ourselves and our generation. We doom ourselves to illness, poverty and ruin. I fear that in focusing upon the needs of the planet, we sometimes forget the needs of our brothers and sisters and our commitment to them.

I am trying to represent the perspective of the many peoples of the earth who struggle, people who can't even imagine the meaning of multinational corporations replacing land agribusiness, or contaminated waste, acid rain and deforestation. When people are hungry and have nowhere to live they are not thinking about the ozone layer or about going to Mars. Talk of futurology seems irrelevant when we're not taking care of the pressing business of here and now. If we care and share now, there is hope for the future.

. . . If we work together to meet the basic needs of the hungry, the homeless, the uneducated, and the alienated then we will be working together in love. . . .

Creation: Since diversity is necessary for the wholeness of the universe what do you feel then is the glue that binds us all together?

Bowman: It has to be love, love that overcomes fear, that shares and makes sure that nobody is hungry, that unites us when we learn about each other, when we share our gifts, when we believe in each other, when we take time to *listen* to each other, and to share our stories, our arts, our customs, our traditions, when we break bread together.

Creation: . . . Are there any other visions or dreams you would like to share with us here?

Bowman: . . . My people have been teaching us about Creation Spirituality for as long as I can remember. We just didn't have a name for it. Respect and love for all of creation; stewardship of the earth and its resources; collaboration and cooperation; appreciation, gratitude, faith, hope and love for all of humankind—basic life-giving, life-sharing values and virtues. Creation Spirituality. We've talked and written about it for so long. Let's live it now, before it's too late.

Healing

Where does the healing come from? It comes when two or three are gathered in Jesus' name and raise their voices in the assembly of the faithful.

Central to Thea's mission in life was healing, making whole. She wanted to heal conflicts, heal the earth, heal inequities, and heal people's spirits. On a September day in 1989, at Saint Stephen's Catholic Church in Minneapolis, Sister Thea celebrated "healing ministry" in a concert for persons of all races living with AIDS and AIDS-related illnesses. The following is a transcription of her words that day.

I have come tonight seeking a blessing. I have come tonight seeking a healing. I don't usually talk about myself, but tonight I want to tell you a little about me. I have cancer. More importantly, I have something in common with my brothers and sisters who have AIDS—weight loss, hair loss, loss of voice, weakness, fatigue, exhaustion.

I'm here tonight to say, God IS. God made me. God loves me. God gave me life, and I want to live as fully as I can live until I die. I want to live my best; I want to love my best; I want to do my best; I want to give my best.

And so tonight I come before you, my brothers, my sisters, my mothers, my fathers, my children. I come before you in my need. I'm standing in the need of prayer.

[Choir and assembly sang "It's Me, O Lord, Standing in the Need of Prayer."]

Let's get in touch with the need tonight, church. Let's be conscious of the need to feel the frustrations, to feel the grief, to feel the sorrow, to feel the pain, and at the same time, to feel the hope and the yearning.

> I pray to God, my father, I pray to Jesus, my brother:
> For people living with AIDS and AIDS-related illnesses,
> For the families and the friends of people living with AIDS
>   and AIDS-related illnesses,
> For the people who are afraid, who avoid, who shun people
>   with AIDS and AIDS-related illnesses,
> For friends who don't know what to say
>   and don't know how to say it,
>   who don't know how to support the ones they love,
> For homeless people with AIDS,
> For the sick ones who come home to die,
> For babies born with AIDS,
> For people, especially young people, who are high-risk,
> For persons awaiting results from AIDS tests
>   and those who are scared to take the test,
> For people who feel they have to deny that they have AIDS:
>   they can't tell friends, they can't even tell their families,
> For people who know the facts and still are careless
>   and irresponsible in their relationships,
> For all our loved ones who are in some way touched,
>   in some way afflicted by AIDS,
> For all my brothers and sisters and fathers and mothers
>   and children standing here tonight,
>   gathered here today,
>   "standing in the need of prayer."
> We offer that need as incense before the throne of God.

[Choir and assembly sang "It's Me, O Lord, Standing in the Need of Prayer."]

We come to prayer because God is our father, and God has promised us everlasting love, everlasting kindness, and everlasting care.

Brothers and sisters, children of our Heavenly Father, let us pray:
Our Father . . .

God is my father, you are my brother, you are my sister.

I'm somebody. I'm somebody special. I'm God's child. I can change things. I can make life better for myself, for my family, for my community, for my church, for the world.

I make life better when I care about somebody, when I reach out and touch somebody, when I smile, when I say yes to life and to laughter and to love and to hope and to joy—even in the midst of troubles.

I make life better when I say yes to God's will as it manifests itself in the circumstances of my life. And I want to say yes to God. I want to say yes to life, yes to hope, yes to love, yes to you, yes to eternity.

[Choir and assembly sang "When I Don't Know Where to Turn" and "I Can Still Say Yes."]

Where does the healing come from? It comes when two or three are gathered in Jesus' name and raise their voices in the assembly of the faithful. We have come to have liturgy tonight, church, and liturgy is the

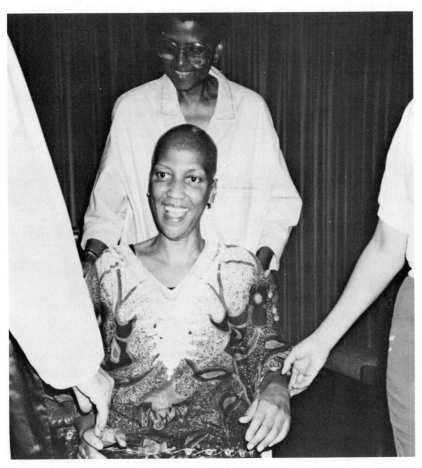

act of the people of God. I'm not talking about the Eucharist. I'm talking about uniting ourselves with heart and voice with the people of God who are suffering all over this world.

When we come together to bless, to consecrate, to reconsecrate this holy ground, we stand, we sit, we love our holy ground, and holy it is because we are here. We are here together.

[Choir and assembly sang "Holy Lord God Almighty, Heaven and Earth Are Full of Your Glory."]

The old lady says, "I go to church, and I lay my burden at the door. I know I'm going to pick it up again, but I come to church because I need me some rest, and I need me some strength." And the young man says, "I got to get my batteries recharged."

Do you feel the energy in this church? The energy is power—it's power to heal, power to give life, to sustain life; it's even power to restore life.

Why should I feel discouraged? Why should the shadows fall? Why should my heart feel lonely when far from home and heaven? Jesus is my portion, my constant friend who watches over me.

[Choir and assembly sang "His Eye Is on the Sparrow."]

The old folks used to say, "You never retire from the service of the Lord." As long as I can take my breath, as long as I have my right mind, I can serve the Lord. As long as I can help somebody, inspire somebody, encourage somebody, reach down and uplift somebody, I can serve the Lord.

What can I do with the time that's left me to help somebody? Sometimes it's just a song, just a tear, just listening with an attentive ear, to help somebody, to teach somebody, to reach somebody, to share laughter, life, love, joy, to leave the world a better place than I happened to find it.

[Choir and assembly sang "If I Can Help Somebody, Then My Living Shall Not Be in Vain."]

There is a balm in Gilead: sharing, caring, giving, helping, giving spiritual care, offering social services, loving and living, and standing in solidarity.

Any time I offer just plain help to somebody—go over there and turn the mattress, go over there and wash the car, go over there and take something to eat, go over there and sit down and hold somebody's hand, go over there when you can't think of anything to say and just be, go over there and ask the questions: What can I do? What do you need?

[Choir sang "There Is a Balm in Gilead."]

If we are to serve, if we are to care, if we are to minister, we have to get right inside. And so let us pray: Spirit, touch me. Touch me with your grace. Touch me with your wisdom. Touch me with your love so that I can help somebody, so that I can serve somebody, so that I can bless somebody. Be the bridge over troubled waters so that I can be the balm in Gilead, be the hands of Jesus stretched out to heal.

[Choir sang "Spirit, Touch Me One More Time."]

Let us pause and remember the one who brought us this far, the one who brought us faith in Jesus, faith in ourselves, faith in family, faith in justice and righteousness, faith in life and laughter, faith in love and life eternal, the one who taught us not to fear death:

> This world is not my home. I'm just passing through.
> I'm going to sit at the welcome table.
> I'm going to drink from the golden fountain.
> I'm going to talk with my king, Jesus.
> There'll be no more weeping and wailing.
> There'll be no more loneliness, pain, and separation.
> There will always be "Howdy, Howdy" and never "Goodbye."

Let us remember all the fathers and mothers, the grandparents, the great grandparents, the foster parents, the godparents, the husbands, the wives, the uncles, the aunts, the sisters, the brothers, the nieces and nephews, the children—all the great people who have brought us this far in faith.

[Choir sang "We've Come This Far by Faith."]

And if we walk on and talk on and work on and pray on and hold on and love on in faith, we shall overcome. Overcome weakness, overcome fatigue, overcome exhaustion, overcome pain and loneliness, overcome frustration, overcome the prejudices and the stereotypes, the anxieties, the grief, the fear, the negative attitudes—all those barriers and boundaries that keep us apart, overcome racism and classism and sexism and materialism, all those "isms" that keep us apart.

[Choir sang "We Shall Overcome."]

Please cross your right arm over your left arm and clasp your neighbor's hands. That means you are going to have to move closer together, and that's part of the program. It's so that when the dogs come, when the bullets come, when the tear gas comes, and when the billy clubs come, and when the tanks come, when the rocks and bricks come, nothing or no one can separate you from your brother, your sister, your father, your mother, your child.

We sing this song in solidarity with our brothers and sisters who are singing it in Japan, in China, in South Africa, in Guatemala, in Nicaragua, in Northern Ireland, all over these United States, wherever men and women and children take a stand for freedom and for justice and for love. . . . We shall live in love.

For all the brothers and sisters with AIDS and AIDS-related illnesses, for their families, for their friends, for those who live with fears and hesitations and anxieties and frustrations, for those who live with a kind of ignorance that leads them to shun, to avoid, that prohibits them from taking care of their own health, for all those who have been touched by this dreadful disease that saps the lives of our communities.

I want to be present. I want to be ready. I want to share what I have—my life, my laughter, my love, my joy. I want to give to you as I receive from you. I want to learn from you. I want my children to learn from you so that we do not repeat the mistakes of the past, so that we can grow together and walk together and talk together and live together in love, in joy, in peace forever.

This little light of mine, I'm going to let it shine.

[Choir and assembly sang "This Little Light of Mine."]

20

How to Celebrate Holy Week

During this Holy Week when Jesus gave his life for love, let us truly love one another.

Several days before her death, Thea dictated this meditation for Holy Week at the request of *Mississippi Today*.

Let us resolve to make this week holy by claiming Christ's redemptive grace and by living holy lives. The Word became flesh and redeemed us by his holy life and holy death. This week especially let us accept redemption by living grateful, faithful, prayerful, generous, just and holy lives.

Let us resolve to make this week holy by reading and meditating holy Scripture. So often we get caught up in the hurry of daily living. As individuals and as families, reserve prime time to be with Jesus, to hear the cries of the children waving palm branches, to see the son of Man riding on an ass's colt, to feel the press of the crowd, to be caught up in the "Hosannas" and to realize how the cries of acclamation will yield to the garden of suffering, to be there and watch as Jesus is sentenced by Pilate to Calvary, to see him rejected, mocked, spat upon, beaten and forced to carry a heavy cross, to hear the echo of the hammer, to feel

---

"How to Celebrate Holy Week" is reprinted from *Mississippi Today* (6 Apr. 1990): 7.

the agony of torn flesh and strained muscles, to know Mary's anguish as he hung three hours before he died.

We recoil before the atrocities of war, gang crime, domestic violence and catastrophic illness. Unless we personally and immediately are touched by suffering, it is easy to read Scripture and to walk away without contacting the redemptive suffering that makes us holy. The reality of the Word falls on deaf ears.

Let us take time this week to be present to someone who suffers. Sharing the pain of a fellow human will enliven Scripture and help us enter into the holy mystery of the redemptive suffering of Christ.

Let us resolve to make this week holy by participating in the Holy Week services of the church, not just by attending (but) by preparing, by studying the readings, entering into the spirit, offering our services as ministers of the Word or Eucharist, decorating the church or preparing the environment for worship. Let us sing, "Lord, have mercy," and "Hosanna." Let us praise the Lord with our whole heart and soul and mind and strength, uniting with the suffering church throughout the world. . . . Let us break bread together, let us relive the holy and redemptive mystery. Let us do it in memory of him, acknowledging in faith his real presence upon our altars.

Let us resolve to make this week holy by sharing holy peace and joy within our families, sharing family prayer on a regular basis, making every meal a holy meal where loving conversations bond family members in unity, sharing family work without grumbling, making love not war, asking forgiveness for past hurts and forgiving one another from the heart, seeking to go all the way for love as Jesus went all the way for love.

Let us resolve to make this week holy by sharing holy peace and joy with the needy, the alienated, the lonely, the sick and afflicted, the untouchable. Let us unite our sufferings, inconveniences and annoyances with the sufferings of Jesus. Let us stretch ourselves, going beyond our comfort zones to unite ourselves with Christ's redemptive work. . . .

During this Holy Week when Jesus gave his life for love, let us truly love one another.

21

Let Me Live Till I Die

I want to say to people just keep on keeping on.

Even after she was stricken by cancer in 1984, Sister Thea was one of the busiest speakers on the Catholic circuit in the United States. Eventually she traveled in a wheelchair, assisted by her friend Sr. Dorothy Ann Kundinger, or "Dort." When Thea lost all her hair because of chemotherapy, she quipped in a letter: "Grooming is surely easier, one swipe with a damp washcloth and a touch of oil for sheen. Sometimes I wear a short wig or my usual African head tie. Sometimes I wear my bald head."

People often asked Sister Thea how she managed to keep going. Her first response would inevitably be, "I try to cope with my mortality," but she would add:

> My early training is part of the ethic that enables me to do that. Old people in the black community taught us that we should serve the Lord until we die. We can even serve the Lord on our deathbeds or in any circumstances in life. If we have faith, hope and love we can pass it on. ("She Inspires Thousands," p. 9)

When Trinity Missionary Fr. John Ford asked his longtime friend what he was to say at her funeral, Sister Thea answered: "Just say what Sojourner Truth said about her own eventual dying. Tell them what Sojourner Truth said: 'I'm not going to die. I'm going home like a shooting star'" ("A Shooting Star," p. 5).

And so she did, on 30 March 1990.

In the year before Thea died, Fabvienen Taylor for *Praying* magazine and Patrice J. Tuohy for *U.S. Catholic* talked to her about living and dying. The following excerpts from the interviews illustrate Thea's rich faith and hope in the face of her own passing.

Taylor: What kind of changes have you had to make in your life because of the cancer?

Bowman: . . . Part of my approach to my illness has been to say I want to choose life, I want to keep going, I want to live fully until I die. . . .

I don't know what my future holds. In the meantime, I am making a conscious effort to learn to live with discomfort, and, at the same time, to go about my work. I find that when I am involved in the business of life, when I'm working with people, particularly with children, I feel better. A kind of strength and energy comes with that.

Taylor: How do you find yourself talking with God about your illness? Has it changed your prayer?

Bowman: I was reared in a community in which prayer was natural . . . consistent, [and] shared. Something good would happen and some old woman would just break out in prayer. Very early, I learned traditional black modalities of prayer—words, symbols, phrases, songs, prayers.

Older folks used to say God is my father and my mother and my sister and brother, my pearl of great price, my lily of the valley, my rock, my sword, my shield. God's a god of peace. God's a god of war. God's water when you're thirsty, bread when you're hungry. God is my doctor, my lawyer, my captain in the battle of life, my friend, my king.

I find that the old prayers come back to me. For example, I recall an old man who would get up in church and say, "I thank you for another day of life because this very night many folks have been laid out on their cooling boards. I ask you for strength to bear the burdens of the day. I know that whatever comes to me is sanctioned by your holy hand." The old styles of prayer bring me comfort.

The excerpts from Fabvienen Taylor's interview with Sister Thea are reprinted from "Lord, Let Me Live Till I Die," *Praying* [Nov.–Dec. 1989]: 19–22.

Taylor: Had you gotten out of the habit of these old prayers?

Bowman: Not, really, but when I'm tired, weak and in pain, I find my-self turning to these prayers quicker than I used to. When I hurt I like to sing some of the old songs: "Precious Lord, take my hand, lead me on, let me stand. I'm tired, I'm weak and I'm worn. Through the storm, through the night, lead me on to the light. Take my hand, Precious Lord, lead me on." I find that prayer and song can take me beyond the pain.

Our old folk would go to church and pray, and they'd come home happy. Within the traditional prayer of the black communi-ty, there were ways of controlling the mind, the mood and even the body, and doing it in Jesus' name. I thank God for that gift of my people. . . .

Our prayer tradition attempts to go to God with feeling and passion and emotion and intensity. I want to be a part of what Jesus felt as he hung on the cross. I want to feel the anguish. I want to feel the love that motivated him to save us. He's the Almighty Word who leapt down from heaven. He's the son of the eternal fa-ther who became human like us in all things save sin. Yet, he ac-cepted the sufferings of a lifetime as a human being to give us life. I want to feel that love, that compassion. . . .

Taylor: Speaking of "keeping on," what's ahead for you now?

Bowman: Life for a while and then death. It's as simple as that. When I first found out I had cancer, I didn't know what to pray for. I didn't know if I should pray for healing or life or death. Then, I found peace in praying for what my folks call "God's perfect will." As it evolved, my prayer has become, "Lord, let me live until I die." By that I mean I want to live, love and serve fully until death comes. If that prayer is answered, if I am able to live until I die, how long really doesn't matter. Whether it's just a few months or a few years is really immaterial.

I grew up with people who believed you could serve the Lord from a sickbed or a deathbed. The great commandment is to love the Lord your God with your whole heart, your whole soul, your whole mind, and all your strength. As long as I have my mental fa-cility, I want to keep on loving. I want to keep on serving. That's what I hope to be about.

My illness has helped me to realize how fragile our hold on life is. I always thought I was going to live to be an old woman, like my mother and my father and all the other old people I knew and was close to when I was a child. But I no longer think that. My time isn't long. Now, I just want to find ways to make the most of the time I have left.

Taylor: How else are you using traditional black prayer in facing the cancer?

Bowman: My people used to say—and still say—sometimes you have to moan. I remember old people sitting out on their porches and moaning on and on in a kind of deep, melodic hum. I've found that moaning is therapeutic. It's a way of centering, the way you do in centering prayer. You concentrate your internal energies and your powers in prayer or wordless outcry to God. Old people used to say the words from Scripture, "When we don't know how to pray the Spirit intercedes for us with inexpressible groaning." So, sometimes you just moan.

Taylor: Do you moan sometimes?

Bowman: Yes, I moan sometimes, I sing sometimes. When I'm sick and don't have the internal resources to pray as I would like, I sing or moan or hum. Because the songs are so familiar, it is an easy way to pray, to unite myself with God. When I have pain, I find it goes away when I hum or sing. . . . It's a lesson I learned from my people and my heritage.

ฅ\ๆ ฅ\ๆ ฅ\ๆ

Tuohy: How do you make sense out of your pain and suffering?

Bowman: I don't make sense of it [suffering]. I try to make sense of life. I try to keep myself open to people and to laughter and to love and to have faith. I try each day to see God's will. I pray, "Oh Jesus, I surrender." I pray, "Father, take this cross away. Not my will, but thy will be done." I console myself with the old Negro spiritual: "Sooner will be done the troubles of this world. I'm going home to live with God."

In the meantime, I take pain medication because I don't want my energies to be absorbed by pain. I want to be able to do what I can do the best that I can.

Tuohy: Is God really present in suffering?

The excerpts from Patrice J. Tuohy's interview with Sister Thea are reprinted from "Sister Thea Bowman: On the Road to Glory," *U.S. Catholic* (June 1990): 21–26.

Bowman: God is present in everything. In the universe, in creation, in me and all that happens to me, in my brothers and sisters, in the church, and in the Eucharist—everywhere. In the midst of suffering, I feel God's presence and cry out to God for help: "Lord, help me to hold on."

Tuohy: Why do people have to suffer? What possible good can come from it?

Bowman: I don't know. Why is there war? Why is there hunger? Why is there pain? Perhaps it's an incentive for struggling human beings to reach out to one another, to help one another, to love one another, to be blessed and strengthened and humanized in the process. Perhaps it's an incentive to see Christ in our world and to view the work of Christ and to feel the suffering of Christ.

I know that suffering gives us new perspective and helps us to clarify our real value. I know that suffering has helped me to clarify my relationships. . . . Perhaps suffering stops us in our tracks and forces us to confront what is real within ourselves and in our environment. . . .

Tuohy: Has your faith changed since you discovered you had cancer?

Bowman: My faith is simpler. In many ways, it's easier; it's closer to home and to reality. I have more desire to grow in faith and hope and love. When I'm in pain, I know I need Jesus to walk with me. I can't make it on my own. I pray, "Lord, I believe. Increase my faith. Help my unbelief."

I remember the words of an old song: "We've come this far by faith, leaning on the Lord, trusting in his words. The Lord has never failed us yet. Oh, can't turn around because we've come this way by faith." . . .

Tuohy: Has your image of God changed?

Bowman: . . . My people graced me with multiple images of the living God.

God is bread when you're hungry, water when you're thirsty, a harbor from the storm. God's a father to the fatherless, a mother to the motherless. God's my sister, my brother, my leader, my guide, my teacher, my comforter, my friend. God's the way-maker and burden-bearer, a heart-fixer and a mind-regulator. God's my doctor who never lost a patient, my lawyer who never lost a case, my chaplain who never lost a battle. God's my all in all, my everything.

God's my rock, my sword, my shield, my lily of the valley, my pearl of great price. God's a god of peace and a god of war. Counselor, Emmanuel, redeemer, savior, Prince of Peace, Son of God, Mary's little baby, wonderful Word of God.

These images come from Scripture and from the meditations of Christians. . . . I meditate on each one of these images on a particular day at a particular time. Each one corresponds to a particular need. All these images help me as I call upon God's name. . . .

Tuohy: Does God seem farther away or closer to you now?

Bowman: God seems closer. I used to feel I could depend upon myself. I used to feel that I could make you a promise and that I could keep a promise. I could tell you that I would be coming to Chicago on a certain date, and I would board a plane and be there. That I might not be able to make the trip would scarcely cross my mind.

I used to say, "It's all in God's hands." But only now do I really know what those words mean because I've experienced them.

I'm so much more grateful than I used to be. I woke up this morning and I could move my legs—I say, "Thank you, God." I woke up this morning and the pain was less than it was a day or two ago—I say, "Thank you, God." I used to take my body for granted.

Tuohy: What other ways have you experienced God's healing?

Bowman: I'm more at peace. I love people. People have love for me. The love they have shown me during my illness, their human love, is somehow a manifestation of the love God bears me. Because I'm sick and needy and dependent, people are more willing to tell me that they love me and I'm more willing to tell them that I love them. The love between us is healing. . . .

Tuohy: What words of encouragement do you have for others who are suffering?

Bowman: I think of these words from an old song: "Hold on just a little while longer. Everything is going to be all right."

To the suffering I say, "Try to reach out to others. Try to let people know how much you love them. Try to maintain a sense of humor and laughter in life. Try to keep in touch with the children and the elderly. Talk about what you're thinking and what you're feeling. Talk about what you need and what you want. Talk about what you see, and talk about your experiences. Invite people to share a prayer with you. Generally, let people know where you are.

Often folks will stand around waiting and wanting to help. Only you, as the sick person, can tell them what they can do."

Tuohy: How can healthy people treat the sick better?

Bowman: It's important for the healthy to listen to the sick. They should ask: "How can I help? What can I do? Would you like me to sit with you a while? What do you need?" . . .

Learn to read the sick. . . . Read the sick person's face and body language. Try to understand where the sick person is coming from. Be sensitive to the need for a quiet and peaceful environment. Don't overload sick people with distractions and noisy actions. Be gentle. . . .

Tuohy: Should Christians fear death?

Bowman: . . . I was taught that death was a part of life; it's going home.

You hear this belief in the old songs: "Swing low, sweet chariot coming for to carry me home." Or "Deep river, my home is over Jordan." Or "Stand still, Jordan: I've got a mother in glory; I've got a father in glory, and I can't stand still." Or the song I sang at my mother's funeral and my father's funeral: "I've done my work; I've sung my song. I've done some good; I've done some wrong. And now I go where I belong. The Lord has willed it so. He knows my heart, and he knows best. He will not harm where he has blessed. And so I go to take my rest where sweet wild roses grow." . . .

Tuohy: Do you find hope in yourself?

Bowman: I know that God is using me in ways beyond my comprehension. God has given me the grace to see some of the seeds that I have sown bear good fruit, and I am so grateful.

Tuohy: Do you ever despair?

Bowman: What for? I don't despair because I believe God leads me and guides me, and I believe that I can reach out for God's hand. I have received such love and so many gifts. That's a part of what I hope at this time in my life to be able to share. I want to say to people just keep on keeping on.

९\७ Select Bibliography ९\७

Other Works by Thea Bowman

"Black History and Culture." *U.S. Catholic Historian* 7, nos. 2 and 3 (Spring–Summer 1989): 307–310.
"Forged by Our History: A Cultural Perspective." *Horizon: Journal of the National Religious Vocation Conference* 15, no. 1 (Fall 1989): 8–12.
"Justice, Power, and Praise." In *Liturgy and Social Justice: Celebrating Rites—Proclaiming Rights*, ed. Edward M. Grosz, pp. 26–39. Collegeville, MN: Liturgical Press, 1989.

Audio and Video Presentations

Almost Home: Living with Suffering and Dying. Liguori, MO: Liguori Publishing Co., 1989. Audiocassette.
Old-Time Religion. Loveland, OH: Treehaus Communications, 1988. Eight programs on four videocassettes.
Sister Thea: Her Own Story. Belleville, IL: Oblate Media and Communications, 1991. Videocassette, 93 mins.
Sister Thea: Round the Glory Manger. Boston: Krystal Records, 1989.
Sister Thea: Songs of My People. Boston: Krystal Records, 1988.

Selected Works About Thea Bowman

Ball, Judy. "A Woman Wrapped in Courage." *Mustard Seed* 6 (Jan. 1989): 1–2.
Bauer, Pam. "Invitation to Sing." *Extension* 78 (Jan. 1984): 5–12.
Bookser-Feister, John. "'I Am Beautiful, You Are Beautiful': Thea Bowman's Ministry of Joy." *St. Anthony Messenger* 93 (July 1985): 29–33.

———. "Sister Thea Teaches Cultural Awareness." *Cornerstone* (Aug. 1985): 38–42.

———. "We Are All Children of God." *Extension* 83 (Apr.–May 1989): 24–27.

Brent, Peggy. "Remembering Sister Thea." *Teaching English in the Two-Year College* 19 (Feb. 1992): 15–17.

Donnelly, Mary Queen. "In Memoriam: Sister Thea Bowman (1937–1990)." *America* (28 Apr. 1990): 420–421.

Fox, Tom. "'Shooting Star' Bowman's Gone Home." *National Catholic Reporter* (13 Apr. 1990): 19.

Francis, Joseph A. "A Sister Who Could Fly Higher Than Any Eagle." *Our Sunday Visitor* (29 Apr. 1990): 19.

Giaimo, Donna William. "A Song in Her Soul." *The Family* (Feb. 1989): 20–22.

Gschwind, Mary Ann. "Bowman, Sister Thea (1937–1990)." In *Black Women in America, An Historical Encyclopedia*. Darlene Clark Hine, ed. Brooklyn, NY: Carlson Publishing, 1993.

Holton, Robert R. "Sister Thea Bowman: Portrait of Faith, Courage." *Our Sunday Visitor* (2 July 1989): 6–7.

Jones, Arthur. "She Sings a Ululu Song That Began in Africa." *National Catholic Reporter* (9 Sept. 1988): 4.

Koontz, Christian, ed. *Thea Bowman: Handing on Her Legacy*. Kansas City, MO: Sheed and Ward, 1991.

McManus, James. "Bishops Help Launch Thea Bowman Foundation." *National Catholic Reporter* (27 Oct. 1989): 3.

O'Connor, John J. "Quintessential Woman." *Catholic New York* (5 Apr. 1990): 5.

"Thea Bowman Foundation Launches $150 Million College Scholarship Fund." *Jet* (6 Nov. 1989): 27.

Acknowledgments (*continued*)

The excerpts by Thea Bowman on pages 11 and 125 are reprinted from "A Shooting Star," *Trinity Missions* (Winter 1990): 5. Used with permission of *Trinity Missions*.

The excerpt on page 11 is reprinted from "New Book Recounts Life of Cherished Nun," by Gayda Hollnagel, *La Crosse Tribune*, 1 Feb. 1992. Used with permission of the author.

The excerpts on pages 17–19 and 125 are reprinted from "She Inspires Thousands, but Who Inspires Her?" *CUA Magazine:* The Catholic University of America (Winter 1990): 7–9. Used with permission.

The excerpt on pages 20–22 is reprinted from "A Woman Wrapped in Courage," by Judy Ball, *Mustard Seed* (Jan. 1989): 1.

The excerpts on pages 25–26 are reprinted from "A Final Farewell to Sister Thea Bowman," *Viterbo Strides* (Fall 1990): 6–7. Used with permission of Viterbo College.

The article on pages 29–37 is reprinted from "To Be Black and Catholic," *Origins* (6 July 1989): 114–118. Used with permission.

The excerpts on pages 38–40, 45–48, and 79–80 are reprinted from "Spirituality: The Soul of the People," *Tell It Like It Is: A Black Catholic Perspective on Christian Education.* (Oakland, CA: National Black Sisters' Conference [NBSC], 1983), pages 84–85; 85, 87–92; and 92–94, respectively. Used with permission of the NBSC.

The excerpt on pages 43–44 and 49–58 are from *Sister Thea: Songs of My People, A Compilation of Favorite Spirituals*, by Thea Bowman (Boston: St. Paul Books and Media, 1989), pages 3, 85, 87–92, and 6–7, 13, 36, 23, 27, 40, 49, 52, 57, 72, 89. Copyright © 1989 by St. Paul Books and Media. Used with permission of St. Paul Books and Media, 50 Saint Paul's Avenue, Boston, MA 02130.

The article by Thea Bowman on pages 59–66 is reprinted from *Lead Me, Guide Me: The African American Catholic Hymnal* (Chicago: G.I.A. Publications, 1987). Copyright © 1987 by G.I.A. Publications. Used with permission of the publisher.

The article by Thea Bowman on pages 70–71 is from "Let the Church Say 'Amen!'" *Extension Magazine* (Mar.–Apr. 1987): 10–11. Used with permission of *Extension Magazine*, published by the Catholic Church Extension Society of the United States of America, 35 East Wacker Drive, Chicago, Illinois 60601.

The excerpts by Thea Bowman on pages 72–75 are taken from *Families: Black and Catholic, Catholic and Black* (Washington, DC: United States Catholic Conference [USCC], 1985), pages 153, 11, 63, and 64. Copyright © 1985 by the USCC, Washington D.C., and used with permission.

The article by Sister Thea Bowman on pages 92–96 is reprinted from "Religious and Cultural Variety: Gift to Catholic Schools," *The Non-Catholic in the Catholic School* (Washington, DC: Department of Religious Education, National Catholic Educational Association [NCEA], 1984 and 1987), pages 20–25. Used with permission of the NCEA.

The excerpts on pages 98–100 are reprinted from "The Message of Music," by Lyn L. Hartmann, *Milwaukee Journal* (17 Jan. 1988). Used with permission of the author.

The speech by Thea Bowman on pages 105–110 is reprinted from *Formation in a New Age: Proceedings of the 1987 Religious Formation National Congress* (Washington, DC: Religious Formation Conference), pages 1–13.

The excerpts on pages 113–116 from Catherine Browning's interview with Thea Bowman are reprinted from "Trusting the Prophetic Call," *Creation* (Nov.–Dec. 1989): 19–21. Used with permission of *Creation* magazine.

The excerpts on pages 126–128 from Fabvienen Taylor's interview with Thea Bowman are from "Lord, Let Me Live Till I Die," *Praying* (Nov.–Dec. 1989): 19–22. Reprinted with permission of *Praying* magazine.

The excerpts on pages 128–132 from Patrice J. Tuohy's interview with Thea Bowman are from "Sister Thea Bowman: On the Road to Glory," *U.S. Catholic* (June 1990): 21–26. Reprinted with permission from *U.S. Catholic,* published by Claretian Publications, 205 West Monroe Street, Chicago, Illinois 60606.